Holly Chantler is an experienced older and vulnerable client solicitor with particular expertise in dealing with complex issues relating to mental capacity, financial abuse, powers of attorney, advance decisions and the Court of Protection (contentious and non-contentious matters). Holly holds a number of professional appointments and qualifications, including as a Court of Protection panel deputy, panel guardian and a director of national organisations Solicitors for the Elderly and the Professional Deputies Forum. She also sits on the Court of Protection Rules Committee and acts as a professional stakeholder for the Ministry of Justice, Office of the Public Guardian and Court of Protection.

A Practical Guide to the Court of Protection

A Practical Guide to the Court of Protection

Holly Chantler

Solicitor and notary public

Law Brief Publishing

Published 2023 by Law Brief Publishing, an imprint of Law Brief Publishing Ltd
30 The Parks
Minehead
Somerset
TA24 8BT

www.lawbriefpublishing.com

Paperback: 978-1-912687-50-3

PREFACE

This practical guide introduces the Court of Protection, an explanation of the relevant legal framework and provides practical support with common applications to the court. The book contains various precedent documents and is the go-to resource for practitioners.

The law described in this book is believed to be correct and up to date as at 28th February 2023.

Holly Chantler
February 2023

CONTENTS

CHAPTER ONE

INTRODUCTION TO THE COURT OF PROTECTION

The Court of a Protection is a distinct court, established by section 45 of the Mental Capacity Act 2005 ("the MCA). It may only make decisions on behalf of someone who lacks capacity or in relation to such a person (known as "P") although in *United Lincolnshire Hospitals NHS Trust v CD* [2019] EWCOP 24 (04 July 2019) the court determined that it has, in exceptional circumstances, the power to make an anticipatory declaration of lawfulness, contingent on P losing capacity, pursuant to section 15(1)(c) MCA.

The Court of Protection is based at First Avenue House, London, but there are also (currently) seven regional hubs and details can be found at www.gov.uk/courts-tribunals/court-of-protection. Contact details for the courts are as follows:

Central Registry
Court of Protection
PO Box 70185
First Avenue House
42-29 High Holborn
London
WC1A 9JA
DX 160013 Kingsway 7
0300 456 4600
courtofprotectionenquiries@justice.gov.uk

North East – East Regional Hub
Leeds Combined Court Centre
The Courthouse
1 Oxford Row
Leeds
LS1 3BG
DX 703016 Leeds 6
0113 306 2800
cop.leeds.countycourt@justice.gov.uk

North East – North Regional Hub
Newcastle Combined Court Centre
Barras Bridge
Newcastle upon Tyne
NE1 8QF
DX 65127 Newcastle upon Tyne 2
0191 205 8750
COPNewcastle.newcastle.countycourt@justice.gov.uk

North West Regional Hub
Manchester Civil Justice Centre
1 Bridge Street West
Manchester
M60 9DJ
DX 724783 Manchester 44
0161 240 5000
COP.Manchester@justice.gov.uk

South East Regional Hub
Reading Court & Family Court
160-163 Friar Street
Reading
RG1 1HE
DX 98010 Reading 6
0118 987 0500
courtofprotection.reading.countycourt@justice.gov.uk

South West Regional Hub
Bristol Civil & Family Justice Centre
2 Redcliff Street
Bristol
BS1 6GR
DX 95903 Bristol 3
0117 366 4830
courtofprotection.bristol.countrycourt@justice.gov.uk

Wales Regional Hub
Cardiff Civil & Family Justice Centre
2 Park Street
Cardiff
CF10 1ET
DX 99500 Cardiff 6
0292 037 6400
Cardiffcop@hmcts.gsi.gov.uk

Midlands Regional Hub
Birmingham Civil and Family Justice Centre
The Priory Courts
33 Bull Street
Birmingham
B4 6DS
DX 701987 Birmingham 7
0121 250 6395
courtofprotection.birmingham.countycourt@justice.gov.uk

Parties involved with Court of Protection proceedings

COP – Court of Protection

Court of Protection visitors – visitors report independently to the Public Guardian, to help them in their role of supervising deputies and investigating concerns about the actions of a deputy or attorney. There are two types of visitors: special visitors (medical practitioners who have specialist knowledge of mental incapacity) and general visitors (who do not need to be medically qualified but must have experience of mental incapacity).

Litigation friend – the role of a litigation friend is to 'direct the proceedings' on behalf of P. This may include instructing a solicitor (and acting on their advice), acting in the best interests of P and complying with any orders of the court.

Official Solicitor – in proceedings before the Court of Protection where P is a party the Official Solicitor may be instructed to act as litigation friend for P. The office of the Official Solicitor includes a number of experienced lawyers who specialise in Court of Protection proceedings.

OPG – The Office of the Public Guardian is an executive agency of the Ministry of Justice. Its responsibility includes supervising deputies and guardians appointed by the courts and taking action where there are concerns about an attorney, deputy or guardian. The OPG is overseen by the Public Guardian (the Public Guardian as at January 2023 is Amy Holmes).

Guidance issued by the Official Solicitor as to when she will act can be found at www.gov.uk/government/publications/appointment-of-the-official-solicitor-in-property-and-affairs-proceedings-practice-note.

The Official Solicitor can be contacted at:

Victory House
30–34 Kingsway
London
WC2B 6EX
DX 141423 Bloomsbury 7
020 3681 2751
Fax: 020 36812762
enquiries@ospt.gov.uk
www.gov.uk/government/organisations/official-solicitor-and-public-trustee

P – the person about whom the proceedings relate

The relationship between the Court of Protection and the Office of the Public Guardian

The Court of Protection and the Office of the Public Guardian are two separate and distinct organisations with limited ability to share information. The OPG has powers of investigation but if it has concerns (particularly if action needs to be taken to consider the ongoing appointment, or removal, of an attorney or deputy), it must make an application to the Court of Protection to deal with the matter.

Powers of the Court of Protection

The Court of Protection has power to make decisions on behalf of a person who lacks capacity or in relation to such a person. The court can exercise its jurisdiction in a number of ways, including to:

- make declarations of capacity (section 15 MCA 2005);
- make one-off decisions on behalf of a person without capacity (sections 16–18 MCA 2005);
- appoint a deputy to make decisions (section 16(2)(b) MCA 2005);
- give directions in respect of lasting powers of attorney ('LPAs') (sections 22 and 23 and Schedule 1 MVA 2005);
- give directions in respect of enduring powers of attorney ('EPAs') (Schedule 4 MCA 2005);

- direct reports from the Public Guardian, Court of Protection Visitor, local authority or NHS body (section 49 MCA 2005); and

- act as a venue for hearing appeals against administrative decisions made under the Deprivation of Liberty Safeguards provisions contained in section 21A and schedule A1 MCA 2005.

The Court's powers to make decisions on P's behalf in respect of property and affairs under section 18 MCA 2005 extend in particular to:

(a) the control and management of P's property;

(b) the sale, exchange, charging, gift or other disposition of P's property;

(c) the acquisition of property in P's name or on P's behalf;

(d) the carrying on, on P's behalf, of any profession, trade or business;

(e) the taking of a decision which will have the effect of dissolving a partnership of which P is a member;

(f) the carrying out of any contract entered into by P;

(g) the discharge of P's debts and of any of P's obligations, whether legally enforceable or not;

(h) the settlement of any of P's property, whether for P's benefit or for the benefit of others;

(i) the execution for P of a will;

(j) the exercise of any power (including a power to consent) vested in P whether beneficially or as trustee or otherwise;

(k) the conduct of legal proceedings in P's name or on P's behalf.

The Court's principal powers in respect of health and welfare are contained in section 17 MCA 2005 and in sections 18 and schedule 2 MCA 2005 in respect of property and financial affairs. All the powers set out in sections 17 and 18 MCA 2005 can be delegated to a deputy apart from those expressly reserved to the Court and set out in section 20. These include:

- the settlement of any of P's property whether for P's benefit or for the benefit of others;
- the execution for P of a Will; or
- the exercise of any power (including a power to consent) vested in P whether beneficially or as a trustee or otherwise.

Section 20 MCA 2005 furthermore sets out additional restrictions appropriate to when a deputy is responsible for welfare matters. Not only must a deputy not act when a person lacks capacity, but the deputy has no authority to:

- prohibit a person from having contact with P;
- direct a person responsible for P's healthcare to allow a different person to take over that responsibility;
- 'refuse consent to the carrying out or continuation of life-sustaining treatment in relation to P'; this is reserved to the Court of Protection;
- restrain P unless the five conditions set out in subsection 20(8)–(13) MCA 2005 are satisfied, that:
    - the deputy is acting within the scope of an express authority;

- P lacks capacity in relation to the matter;
- the deputy reasonably believes that the restraint is necessary to prevent harm to P;
- the restraint is proportionate to the likelihood of P suffering harm and the seriousness of that harm; and
- the act of restraint does not amount to a deprivation of liberty.

Whilst the court's powers are wide, there are limitations to its authority:

- any decision made by a body or person on behalf of another person who lacks capacity must be made in that person's best interests (sections 1, 4 and 16(3) MCA 2005);
- the court (and a deputy appointed by the court) can only act in respect of decisions a person lacks capacity to make (sections 16(1) and 20(1) MCA 2005);
- decisions made by the court should where possible be the least restrictive and limited (sections 1(6) and 16(4) MCA 2005);
- decisions can only be made on behalf of a person who is over 18 – however, if P is under the age of 16, the court can make decisions in respect of property and affairs if it considers it likely that P will still lack capacity to make decisions in respect of the matter in question when P reaches 18 (section 18(3) MCA 2005);
- certain decisions such as consenting to marriage or sexual relationships, voting in an election or consenting to treatment for mental disorder are beyond the scope of the MCA 2005 (sections 27–29 MCA 2005).

Principles of the Mental Capacity Act 2005

All decisions made on behalf of or in respect of a person who lacks capacity, must be made pursuant to the principles of the MCA, as set out in section 1. These principles are:

1. A person must be assumed to have capacity unless it is established that he lacks capacity.

2. A person it not to be treated as unable to make a decision unless all practicable steps to help him to do so have been taken without success.

3. A person is not to be treated as unable to make a decision merely because he makes an unwise decision.

4. An act done or decision made under the MCA for or on behalf of a person who lacks capacity must be done, or made, in his best interests.

5. Before the act is done, or the decision is made, regard must be had as to whether the purpose for which it is needed can be as effectively achieved in a way that is less restrictive of the person's rights and freedom of action.

<u>Mental capacity</u>

For the purposes of the MCA 2005, there is a two-stage test of capacity.

The first stage, as set out in section 2 MCA 2005, states that "a person lacks capacity in relation to a matter if at the material time, he is unable to make a decision for himself in relation to the matter because of an impairment of, or a disturbance in the functioning of, the mind or brain".

It does not matter whether the impairment or disturbance is permanent or temporary and there does not need to have been any formal diagnosis.

A lack of capacity cannot be established merely by reference to:

- A person's age or appearance, or
- A condition of his or an aspect of his behaviour, which might lead others to make unjustified assumptions about his capacity.

The test of capacity is on the balance of probabilities. That is, whether a person is more likely that not to lack capacity to make the decision in question.

The second stage of the test of capacity is set out in section 3 MCA 2005 and this states that for the purposes of section 2, a person is unable to make a decision for him or herself if he or she is unable to:

- Understand the information relevant to the decision (which also includes the reasonably foreseeable consequence of deciding one way or another or making no decision at all).
- Retain that information.
- Use or weigh that information as part of the process of making the decision or
- Communicate his decision (whether by talking, using sign language or any other means).

That fact that a person is able to retain the information relevant to a decision for a short period only does not prevent him from being regarded as able to make the decision in question.

Section 3 MCA 2005 requires the person to understand the information relevant to the decision. The relevant information depends on the decision in question and can be determined by reference to case law. Specific tests of capacity are set out in the following section.

The fourth principle of the MCA 2005 states that any decision made on behalf of or in respect of a person who lacks capacity must be made in their best interests. Section 4 MCA 2005 sets out some of the factors to be considered when making a best interests decision. Although no factor carries more weight than any other, consideration of P's past and present wishes and feelings is very important.

Any application to the Court of Protection needs to demonstrate how it is in P's best interests for the order to be made.

CHAPTER TWO

SPECIFIC TESTS OF CAPACITY: THE INFORMATION RELEVANT TO THE DECISION

The definition and test of capacity as set out in the MCA 2005 apply 'for the purposes of this Act'. There are several common law tests of capacity established before the MCA and these continue to apply in those specific circumstances (including capacity to make a will, enter into marriage, gift, contract and litigate).

Identifying the specific decision in question, and the information relevant to making the decision, is not always straightforward (see for example *Re S: D v R (Deputy of S) and S* [2010] EWHC 4505 (COP) but the common tests of capacity are set out below.

As mentioned above, part of the general test of capacity is to understand the reasonably foreseeable consequences of deciding one way or another or making no decision at all. This can be particularly difficult in relation to personal welfare decisions. The Supreme Court in *A Local Authority v JB* [2021] UKSC 52 confirmed that the reasonable consequences are to not be limited only to the consequences for P, but can also extend to the consequences for others.

Capacity to make a lasting power of attorney – *Re Collis* [2010] COP 27/10/10 (unreported)

The test of capacity as set out in the MCA 2005 provides the framework in relation to capacity to execute a lasting power of attorney ("LPA"). Relevant information should include information about the consequences of not executing an LPA.

In his judgment in *Re Collis*, Senior Judge Lush considered the difference between capacity needed to make an enduring power of attorney ("EPA") and an LPA (lasting powers of attorney were introduced by the Mental Capacity Act 2005 and replaced EPAs. EPAs made before 1 October 2007 remain valid but new ones could not be made after that date). The Senior Judge stated "the criteria in Re K, Re F are not entirely applicable to LPAs because of some fairly major differences between EPAs and LPAs, and would need to be adapted in several respects. For example:

- The donor would need to understand that the LPA cannot be used until it is registered by the Public Guardian. This is simply not the case with an EPA.

- One would expect to see a change of emphasis between the creation of an LPA for personal welfare and an LPA for property and affairs; and, in particular, the donor would need to understand that the attorney under an LPA for personal welfare can only make decisions that the donor is contemporaneously incapable of making for him- or herself.

- Unlike an EPA, the donor can revoke an LPA at any time when he or she has the capacity to do so (section 19(2)), without the court having to confirm the revocation.

- The authority conferred by an LPA, unlike an EPA, is subject to the provisions of the Mental Capacity Act 2005 and, in particular, section 1 (the principles) and section 4 (best interests) (section 9(4)).

- The statutory definition of capacity in section 3(4) of the Act specifically requires the donor to be aware of the foreseeable consequences of not executing an LPA, whereas in Re K, Re F Mr Justice Hoffmann did not include an understanding of the effect of not making an EPA in his summary of the matters which should ordinarily be explained to the donor".

As noted above in relation to the professional obligations of legal practitioners, the Senior Judge preferred the contemporaneous evidence of the solicitor who acted as certificate provider when considering the capacity of the donor. A certificate provider is required to confirm that the donor of the LPA at the time the LPA is signed:

- the donor understands the purpose of the LPA and the scope of the authority conferred under it;
- no fraud or undue pressure is being used to induce the donor to create the LPA;
- there is nothing else which would prevent this LPA from being created by the completion of the instrument.

Notwithstanding the Senior Judge's determination in this case, legal practitioners should always consider obtaining a specific medical report particularly where there are concerns about the client's capacity or other reasons which may lead to a dispute.

Capacity to manage property and financial affairs – *A, B and C v X, Y* [2012] EWHC 2400 (COP)

In his judgment, Hedley J noted (at 41) "the general concept of managing affairs is an ongoing act and, therefore, quite unlike the specific act of making a will or making an enduring power of attorney. The management of affairs relates to a continuous state of affairs whose demands may be unpredictable and may occasionally be urgent".

Whether someone lacks capacity to manage his property and affairs will depend on the individual circumstances. More complex affairs will require a higher level of mental capacity. It is imperative to differentiate between various decisions to be made and that a client may be able to make some of these decisions, on some occasions, but not others.

Capacity to litigate – *Masterman-Lister v Jewell* [2002] EWCA Civ 1889

In *Masterman-Lister v Jewell*, the Court of Appeal identified the key question as being whether "a party to legal proceedings is capable of understanding, with the assistance of such proper explanation (in broad terms and simple language) from legal advisers and other experts as the case may require, the matter on which their consent or decision was likely to be necessary in the course of those proceedings" (paragraph 75). Furthermore (at paragraph 79), " a person should not be held unable to understand the information relevant to a decision if he can understand and explanation of that information in broad terms and simple language; and that he should not be regarded as unable to make a rational decision merely because the decision which he does, in fact, make is a decision which would not be made by a person on ordinary prudence".

The test applies to the proceedings as a whole and not at each step in the conduct of the proceedings. This was confirmed in *Dunhill v Burgin* [2014] UKSC 18.

As has already been emphasised, capacity is time and matter specific: the litigant must have capacity to conduct the particular proceedings with which they are involved, the ability to conduct other proceedings or make decisions in general is not relevant (*Sheffield City Council v E and another* [2005] Fam 326).

As noted by Mr Justice Mostyn in *Re P* [2021] EWCOP 27, "conducting litigation is not simply a question of providing instructions to a lawyer and the sitting back and watching the case unfold. Litigation is a heavy-duty, dynamic transactional process both prior to and in court, with information to be recalled, instructions to be given, advice to be received and decisions to be taken, on many occasions, on a number of issues, over the span of the proceedings as they develop: *TB and KB v LH (Capacity to Conduct Proceedings)* [2019] EWCOP 14". As such, the level of capacity required to conduct litigation is set relatively high.

Furthermore, Mr Justice Mostyn stated that, in his opinion, a litigant needs the same level of capacity to conduct litigation whether she is represented or not [paragraph 31].

When considering whether a client has capacity to conduct proceedings, consider whether they can:

- understand how the proceedings are to be funded
- understand the possibility of not succeeding and the risk of having to pay costs
- make the types of decisions which arise in litigation
- give proper instructions for, and approve the particulars of a claim, and approve a compromise

For a client to have capacity to agree a compromise, they would need:

- insight into the compromise
- an ability to instruct solicitors to advise them on it
- an understanding of the solicitor's advice
- to be able to weight that advice before making a decision

Capacity to gift – Re *Beaney* [1978] 2 All ER 595

The common law test of capacity to gift as set out in *Re Beaney* continues to apply. In *Re Beaney* it was stated, "the degree or extent of understanding required in respect of any instrument is relative to the particular transaction which it is to effect … in the case of … a gift inter vivos … the degree required varies with the circumstances of the transaction. Thus where at one extreme the subject matter and value of the gift are trivial in relation to the donor's other assets a low degree of understanding will suffice. But, at the other extreme, if its effect is to dispose of the donor's only asset of value and thus ... to pre-empt the devolution of his estate ... then the degree of understanding required is as high as that required for a will, and the donor must understand the claims of all potential donees and the extent of the property to be disposed of" (Sir Martin Nourse QC).

The High Court in *Kicks v Leigh* [2014] EWHC 3926 (Ch) confirmed that the common law test is the correct test.

To engage in social media – *Re A (Capacity: Social Media and Internet Use: Best Interests)* [2019] EWCOP 2 (February 2019)

Mr Justice Cobb determined that the issue as to whether someone has capacity to engage in social media for the purposes of online contact is distinct from the consideration of other forms of direct or indirect contact. He was also satisfied that wider internet use is different to general issues surrounding care. He identified particular characteristics of social media networking and internet use which distinguish it from other forms of contact and care, which include significant scope for harassment, bullying, exposure to harmful content, sexual grooming exploitation (in its many forms), encouragement of self-harm, access to dangerous individuals and/or information.

The relevant information under section 3(1)(a) MCA P needs to be able to understand, retain and use and weigh to be able to make a decision is:

(i) information and images (including videos) which you share on the internet or through social media could be shared more widely, including with people you don’t know, without you knowing or being able to stop it;

(ii) it is possible to limit the sharing of personal information or images (and videos) by using ‘privacy and location settings’ on some internet and social media sites;

(iii) if you place material or images (including videos) on social media sites which are rude or offensive, or share those images, other people might be upset or offended;

(iv) some people you meet or communicate with ('talk to') online, who you don't otherwise know, may not be who they say they are ('they may disguise, or lie about, themselves'); someone who calls themselves a 'friend' on social media may not be friendly;

(v) some people you meet or communicate with ('talk to') on the internet or through social media, who you don't otherwise know, may pose a risk to you; they may lie to you, or exploit or take advantage of you sexually, financially, emotionally and/or physically; they may want to cause you harm;

(vi) if you look at or share extremely rude or offensive images, messages or videos online you may get into trouble with the police, because you may have committed a crime.

Mr Justice Cobb added the following points to assist in its interpretation and application:

i) in relation to (ii) above, [he did] not envisage that the precise details or mechanisms of the privacy settings need to be understood but P should be capable of understanding that they exist, and be able to decide (with support) whether to apply them;

ii) in relation to (iii) and (vi) above, [Mr Justice Cobb used] the term 'share' in this context as it is used in the 2018 Government Guidance: 'Indecent Images of Children: Guidance for Young People': that is to say. "sending on an email, offering on a file sharing platform, uploading to a site that other people have access to, and possessing with a view to distribute";

iii) in relation to (iii) and (vi) above, [Mr Justice Cobb chose] the words 'rude or offensive' – as these words may be easily understood by those with learning disabilities as including not only the insulting and abusive, but also the sexually explicit, indecent or pornographic;

iv) in relation to (vi) above, this is not intended to represent a statement of the criminal law, but is designed to reflect the importance, which a capacitous person would understand, of not searching for such material, as it may have criminal content, and/or steering away from such material if accidently encountered, rather than investigating further and/or disseminating such material. Counsel in this case cited from the Government Guidance on 'Indecent Images of Children' (see (ii) above). Whilst the Guidance does not refer to 'looking at' illegal images as such, a person should know that entering into this territory is extremely risky and may easily lead a person into a form of offending. This piece of information (in [28](vi)) is obviously more directly relevant to general internet use rather than communications by social media, but it is relevant to social media use as well.

Mr Justice Cobb added that whilst he had considered whether to include the potentially psychologically harmful impact on the user, he took the view that many capacitous internet users do not specifically consider this risk, or if they do, they are indifferent to the risk and he therefore did not think it was appropriate to include it in the list of information relevant to the test of capacity.

To engage in sexual relations – *A Local Authority v JB (by his litigation friend, the Official Solicitor)* [2021] UKSC 52

Guidance was given by the Court of Appeal in *A Local Authority v JB (Rev 2) [2020] EWCA Civ 735 (11 June 2020)* as to the information relevant to a decision whether to engage in sexual relations.

"…

100 In summary, when considering whether, as a result of an impairment of, or disturbance in the functioning of, the mind or brain, a person is unable to understand, retain, or use or weigh information relevant to a decision whether to engage in sexual relations, the information relevant to the decision may include the following:

(1) the sexual nature and character of the act of sexual intercourse, including the mechanics of the act;

(2) the fact that the other person must have the capacity to consent to the sexual activity and must in fact consent before and throughout the sexual activity;

(3) the fact that P can say yes or no to having sexual relations and is able to decide whether to give or withhold consent;

(4) that a reasonably foreseeable consequence of sexual intercourse between a man and woman is that the woman will become pregnant;

(5) that there are health risks involved, particularly the acquisition of sexually transmitted and transmissible infections, and that the risk of sexually transmitted infection can be reduced by the taking of precautions such as the use of a condom.

101 There remains the question whether the information relevant to the decision whether to engage in sexual relations must always include all of the matters identified in the previous paragraph.

102 This is clearly a matter of considerable importance. In *NB*, Hayden J held that an assessment of the information relevant

to a decision to have sexual relations requires the incorporation of P's circumstances and characteristics according to the facts of the particular case. *NB* was not the first case in which this approach was adopted. As illustrated above, it was an approach I adopted myself in *Re TZ* when I observed in passing that the relevant information included the risks of pregnancy "if the relations are heterosexual".

103 It is important to note, however, that the question whether the information relevant to the decision whether to engage in sexual relations must always include all of the matters identified in paragraph 100 above does not arise on the present appeal. Any observations we might make on the subject would therefore not be binding authority. The summary of the case law set out above illustrates that on several occasions judicial obiter dicta in this difficult area of the law have been initially followed by other judges, only to be rejected in later cases after hearing further argument. For that reason, it would be prudent for this Court to refrain from commenting until it has an opportunity to hear full argument on the point in a case where the issue arises on the appeal."

Although the judgment was appealed, the Supreme Court agreed with the Court of Appeal that the information relevant to a decision to engage in sex includes (1) the fact that the other person must have the ability to consent to the sexual activity and (2) the fact that the other person must in fact consent before and throughout the sexual activity.

To execute a will – Banks v Goodfellow [1870] LR 5 QB 549

The long-standing test of capacity at common law is that set out in *Banks v Goodfellow* [1870] LR 5 QB 549, the test being that "it is essential to the exercise of such a power [i.e. to make a will] that the testator:

1. shall understand the nature of the act and its effects;

2. shall understand the extent of the property of which he is disposing;

3. shall be capable to comprehend and appreciate the claims to which he ought to give effect; and

4. with a view to the latter object, that no disorder of the mind shall poison his affections, pervert his sense of right, or prevent the exercise of his natural faculties – that no insane delusions shall influence his will in disposing of his property and bring about the disposal of it which, if the mind had been sound, would not have been made".

To these four tests, a fifth was arguably added by Mr Justice Briggs in *Key v Key* [2010] EWHC 408 which extended the *Banks v Goodfellow* test by taking into account the decision-making powers of the testator as a whole.

The *Banks v Goodfellow* test has recently been upheld as the applicable law in *Re Clitheroe* [2021] 1102 (Ch).

There are two primary stages at which capacity is assessed:

1. when instructions are provided (which may be on more than one occasion)

2. when the will is executed

It is possible for the testator's capacity to have deteriorated between providing instructions and executing the will. In *Parker v Felgate* (1883) 8 PD 171, it was established that the test of capacity at the time the will is signed is as follows:

1. when the will is executed, does the testator remember and understand the instructions given to their solicitor?

2. is the testator capable of understanding each clause of the will if it was explained to them?

3. is the testator capable of understanding, and do they understand, that they are executing a will for which they had previously given instructions to their solicitor?

If the answer to any of the questions is yes, the will is valid. This principle has been further applied in cases such as *Clancy v Clancy* [2003] EWHC 1885 (Ch) and *Perrins v Holland* [2010] EWCA Civ 840. It has also been applied in relation to lifetime gifts on the basis the same underlying reasons for the decision apply to lifetime dispositions as well as on death (*Singellos v Singellos* [2010] EWHC 2353 (Ch)).

The MCA does not replace the common law test of capacity to make a will and this was confirmed in a number of post-MCA cases including *Scammell v Farmer* [2008] EWHC 1100 (Ch) and *Walker v Badmin* [2014] All ER (D) 258 where the judge dealt specially with the issue as to which test of capacity should apply, confirming it was the common law test and not the MCA. The MCA Code of Practice at paragraphs 4.32 and 4.33 confirms that the MCA definition of capacity reflects the common law test and does not replace it. It can, however, be argued that the MCA definition of capacity is wider than that in *Banks v Goodfellow*.

A person's capacity to make a will must be considered as a distinct decision and it is possible that a client may lack capacity to manage their property and affairs but does have capacity to make a will (see *A, B and C v X, Y* [2012] EWHC 2400 (COP)).

Although *Banks v Goodfellow* continues to be the authoritative law on testamentary capacity, the MCA test of capacity applies to statutory wills.

CHAPTER THREE

WHEN AN APPLICATION TO THE COURT OF PROTECTION MAY BE REQUIRED

There are many reasons why an application to the Court of Protection may be required, the most common of which are:

- when a person does not have a valid enduring power of attorney or lasting power of attorney;
- where the attorney is restricted within the power of attorney from taking a particular action;
- where an attorney is conflicted and requires court consent (such as obtaining agreement to equity release where they are the co-owner with the donor;
- applications for regular payments from P's assets to the deputy or attorney in respect of remuneration;
- applications in relation to the sale of property owned by P, where the sale is non-contentious;
- applications for authority to disclose information as to P's assets, state of health or other circumstances;
- applications to make a gift or loan from P's assets;
- applications to sell or otherwise deal with P's investments;

- applications for authority to apply for a grant of probate or representation, where P would be the person entitled to the grant but for P's lack of capacity;

- applications relating to the lease or grant of a tenancy in relation to property owned by P;

- applications to arrange an overdraft or bank loan on P's behalf;

- applications to authorise a sale of P's property to the attorney or donee, or a family member of P, the attorney or donee, at proper market value, and provided that the market value of the property in question is not disproportionately large when compared to the size of P's estate as a whole;

- applications for authority to obtain a copy of P's will;

- applications for the approval of equity releases;

- applications for the removal of a deputy;

- applications seeking authorisation to commence, continue or defend litigation on behalf of P;

- applications for the settlement of P's property, whether for P's benefit or for the benefit of others;

- applications to vary the terms of a trust or estate in which P has an interest;

- applications for a statutory will or codicil; and

- applications to operate or cease to operate a business belonging to P, or to dissolve a partnership of which P is a member.

CHAPTER FOUR

COMMON APPLICATIONS TO THE COURT OF PROTECTION

The most common applications to the Court of Protection are set out below.

Appointment of a property and affairs deputy

If the client lacks capacity to manage his or her affairs, it may be necessary for a third party to be authorised to manage them on their behalf. The client may have already made provision for such circumstances by making an EPA or LPA. In the event no such provision has been made, or the provision is no longer relevant or applicable (for example if the attorney has died), it may be necessary for an application to be made to the Court of Protection for a deputy to be appointed.

Who may be a deputy

No one has the right to be appointed as deputy; it is a decision of the court to make the appointment on the basis of P's best interests. Often it will be a close relative but there may be circumstances when that person or persons will not be appropriate, perhaps due to concerns about their ability to carry out the role or the complexity of P's affairs. If there is no appropriate family member willing and able to act, the appointment may be for a friend, solicitor (including trust corporations Appointment of trust corporations – *Trust Corporations: Various Incapacitated Persons and the Appointment of Trust Corporations as Deputies* [2018] EWCOP 3) or other professional advisor or an officer of the local social services (see *Re SH* [2018] EWCOP 21)).

Section 19 MCA 2005 sets out who may be appointed as a deputy. A prospective deputy must be over 18 and consent to the appointment. Deputies can be appointed to act solely, jointly or jointly and severally. In practice, a joint appointment is likely to be unworkable. It is also possible for the court to make provision for the appointment of a successor deputy, although this is rare in practice as the court prefers to assess the suitability of the deputy at the time they are appointed. *Re H, F and M* [2015] EWCOP 52 is an example of where a successor deputy was appointed.

Professional deputies should carefully consider whether they wish (or indeed would be covered by their professional indemnity insurance) to act as a co-deputy with a lay deputy, particularly where the application is on a joint and several basis as co-deputies may remain liable for the action or actions of their co-deputy.

The duties of a deputy

Before accepting the role of deputy, a prospective deputy should carefully consider and understand the nature and extent of his duties, the Deputy's Declaration (form COP4) which accompanies an application for the appointment of a deputy, sets out various personal undertakings which the prospective deputy is required to give. These emphasise the core fiduciary duties of the deputy as well as the deputy's wider duties under MCA 2005. Useful further guidance can be found in the MCA Code of Practice, the guidance provided by the Court of Protection at https://www.gov.uk/become-deputy and the Office of the Public Guardian's deputy standards https://www.gov.uk/government/publications/office-of-the-public-guardian-deputy-standards.

The application process

An application for the appointment of a property and affairs deputy must be made in accordance with part 9 of the Court of Protection Rules 2017, as supplemented by Practice Direction 9H – Property and Affairs Deputyship Applications. This book is limited to property and affairs applications but as a starting point, if the application is for the appointment of a personal welfare deputy, forms COP1, COP1B, COP3 and COP4 must be used. It may also be appropriate for a COP24 to be filed.

The application is made using forms COP1, COP1A, COP3 and COP4 and these should be submitted to the Court of Protection, together with the application fee of £371. Depending on P's financial circumstances, an exemption or remission of this fee may be available.

The COP3, Assessment of Capacity form, should be completed by a professional medical practitioner, such as a GP, Psychiatrist or Mental Health Professional. If there is any doubt about P's capacity or there is any prospect of an objection being raised to the application, the COP3 should be completed by a specialist psychiatrist, psycho-geriatrician or similarly other qualified consultant experienced in assessing cognitive impairment and mental capacity. If there is any doubt about P's capacity and the COP3 has been completed by a General Practitioner or Health professional, and a subsequent objection is raised, it is likely that the Court will require a Specialist Capacity Assessment to be carried out and as such, it is preferable to submit this at the outset.

<u>Notice to P</u>

Before filing the application with the Court of Protection, the applicant must first notify P that the application is to be made using notification form COP14PADep which provides the following information:

a. who the applicant is;

b. that the application raises the question of whether P lacks capacity in relation to a matter or matters and what that means;

c. what will happen if the court makes an order or direction that has been applied for;

d. details of the person it is proposed should be appointed to make decisions on behalf of P in relation to their property and affairs;

e. that P may seek advice and assistance in relation to the application;

f. that P may complete and return the form to the person notifying them to acknowledge notification and indicate their wishes and feelings about the application;

g. that the notification form must be returned to the applicant before the end of 14 days from the date P received it, and if it is not sent within this period the court will assume that P does not object;

h. that P may, in addition to sending the completed form back to the applicant, send a copy of it to the court;

i. that at the point the application is made, the applicant will be required to provide to the court a copy of the notification form if it has been completed and returned to the applicant; and

The COP14PADep also contains a section to be completed by the person who personally notifies P, to record the steps taken to explain the application to P, the extent to which they understood or appeared to understand and any response they gave and any wishes and feelings P expressed about the application.

Persons to notify

Before the application is made, it is also necessary to give notice to any proposed respondent and to the persons to be notified (being those persons who are required to be notified as specified in Practice Direction 9B) that an application is to be made. Those persons are:

(a) spouse or civil partner;

(b) person who is not a spouse or a civil partner but who has been living with P as if they were;

(c) parent or guardian;

(d) child;

(e) brother or sister;

(f) grandparent or grandchild;

(g) aunt or uncle;

(h) child of a person falling within sub-paragraph (e);

(i) step-parent; and

(j) half-brother or half-sister.

It is necessary for at least three persons to be notified. If there is more than one person within a class, they must all be notified even if that means more than three being notified in total. In the event that there are not three persons from the list above (or if it is considered appropriate to notify them in any case), consider notifying P's close friends, GP, consultant or care home manager.

One of the most common reasons for rejection of deputy applications is because insufficient persons have been notified.

Notification should be given using form COP15PADep, which provides the following information:

a. who the applicant is;

b. Details about the person to whom the application relates (p);

c. Details of the application being made and the order or orders sought;

d. The full name and address of the person being notified and their connection to p;

e. That the person notified is asked to complete the form and return it to the application no more than 14 days after receiving it, to acknowledge notification and to indicate whether they consent or object to the application;

f. That the person may, in addition to sending the completed form back to the applicant, send a copy of it to the court; and

g. That at the point an application is made, the applicant is required to provide to the court all completed notification forms where these have been returned to the application within the prescribed time.

Responding to an application

The person to whom the application relates may complete the COP14PADep and the applicant must return it to the court.

A person notified of the application should complete the notification form COP15PADep and return it to the application within 14 days from the date of receipt, indicating whether they consent or object to the proposed application. They can also file a copy of the form directly with the court.

Non-response

If no COP14PADep or COP15PADep is returned within 14 days of receipt, the applicant can make the application with a declaration that no response has been received. The court will infer that no objection has been raised.

Filing the application

The applicant must not file the application with the court until either:

a. they have received acknowledgement of notification from all persons notified, or

b. the end of 14 days after the latest notification was provided to P or the other persons to be notified.

Where the application has not been made within three months after first notification of any person, new notification must be provided.

To file an application using the online portal, the applicant must:

a. complete the form in the online portal, providing the following information which is signed with a statement of truth and an acknowledgement that the court may contact any of the persons listed:

    (i) the date on which P was notified and steps taken to enable P to understand the information;

    (ii) details of any wishes and feelings expressed by P about the application;

    (iii) details of the people notified that the application was going to be made, and their relationship to P;

    (iv) the dates on which each person was notified or an explanation as to why they have not been notified;

(v) whether the persons notified consent or object to the application or have not responded;

(vi) upload all completed acknowledgment of notification forms received;

(vii) upload all supporting documents as required by Rule 9.4 and Practice Direction 9A; and

(viii) pay the appropriate court fee (with professional users using Payment by Account (PBA) where possible).

To file an application by post, the applicant must file with the court:

a. the completed COP1 which is signed with a statement of truth and an acknowledgement that the court may contact any of the persons listed:

   (i) details of the people notified that the application was going to be made, and their relationship to P;

   (ii) the dates on which each person was notified or an explanation as to why they have not been notified;

   (iii) whether the persons notified consent or object to the application or have not responded; and

b. the completed COP14PADep providing the date on which P was notified, steps taken to enable P to understand the application, and any wishes and feelings expressed by P about the application;

c. all completed acknowledgement of notification forms received;

d. all supporting documents as required by Rule 9.4 and Practice Direction 9A; and

e. pay the appropriate court fee (with professional users using Payment by Account (PBA) where possible).

It is relatively unusual to include anyone as a respondent to the application. This is more relevant during ongoing contested proceedings.

The Court will notify the applicant that the order has been made but before copies of the order are released, the Court will usually require the deputy to obtain a security bond. This is a form of insurance policy and is used to protect P and his or her estate.

The Court will set the level of bond by reference to various factors and guidance about this can be found in the two judgments of *Baker v H* [2009] EWHC B31 (Fam) and *The Public Guardian v Matrix Deputies and the London Borough of Enfield and others* [2017] EWCOP 17, as well as in the Public Guardian's Guidance SD15 (which was published in 2015).

The bond premium is paid annually and the deputy should review the level of cover, making an application to the Court for reconsideration (both to increase and decrease the level of cover) if appropriate. The bond must usually be paid for before the order is released.

On receipt of the order, P must be notified in person for a second time, although it is usual for formal confirmation of notification to the court to be dispensed with.

It is necessary to check the terms of the order carefully, noting any restrictions on the authority of the deputy. One common restriction is regarding the disposal or acquisition of property on P's behalf. An application for reconsideration of the order should be made using form COP9 within 21 days of the Order being served.

The Public Guardian is responsible for the supervision of deputies. An initial deputy assessment fee of £100 is usually payable and ongoing supervision fees of £320 or £35 are paid annually from P's estate, depending on P's circumstances.

Deputies are required to submit an annual report to the Office of the Public Guardian using form OPG102, which can be completed online or print. This sets out details of the decisions made by the deputy during the previous year, as well as recording financial transactions.

Professional deputies are also required to estimate their fees for the next reporting period using form OPG105. Solicitors should continually review the estimate given in the OPG105 and in the event that they anticipate exceeding it by 20% or more, they should notify the Office of the Public Guardian accordingly. Failure to do so risks not being able to recover the additional costs.

Appointment of a deputy: summary

Pre-application	Upfront notification to P and notifiable persons
Application	File with the Court of Protection online or by post: - COP1 - COP1A - COP3 - Fee
Once the order has been made	Pay the premium bond Notify P
Anniversary of the order	File with the Office of the Public Guardian: - OPG105 - OPG102

Exercising trustee powers

A deputy cannot exercise trustee powers (section 20(3)(c) MCA 2005) and an attorney acting under an enduring power of attorney or lasting power of attorney can only exercise trustee powers in limited circumstances (principally only in relation land).

Where a trustee lacks capacity to act in that capacity, the process to remove them, and potentially replace them, will depend on a number of factors.

P has the power to appoint and/or retire trustees under the settlement or their consent is required – section 18(1)(j) MCA 2005

The starting point will be to consider whether the trust instrument contains any express provisions as to what is to happen if a trustee lacks capacity. Where the power of appointment and/or retirement is with the incapacitated trustee, an order of the Court of Protection will usually be required pursuant to section 18 MCA 2005 (who will also make consequential vesting or other orders).

Removal of an incapacitated trustee where no replacement required – section 39 Trustee Act 1925

Section 39 Trustee Act 1925 states "where a trustee is desirous of being discharged from the trust, and after his discharge there will be either a trust corporation or at least two to act as trustees to perform the trust, then, if such trustee as aforesaid by deed declares that he is desirous of being discharged from the trust, and if his co-trustees and such other person, if any, as is empowered to appoint trustees, by deed consent to the discharge of the trustee, and to the vesting in the co-trustees alone of the trust property, the trustee desirous of being discharged shall be deemed to have retired from the trust, and shall, by the deed, be discharged therefrom under this Act, without any new trustee being appointed in his place".

As such, where an incapacitated trustee does not need to be replaced, an application can be made to the Court of Protection to exercise P's right to retire and be discharged from the trust pursuant to section 39 Trustee Act 1925. The application will be for "the deputy to be authorised in the name and on behalf of P to exercise the power vested in P of retiring from the trusts [as described] and for such purpose to execute such deeds as may be necessary".

Where P is a trustee with a beneficial interest and there is another trustee – section 36(9) Trustee Act 1925

Section 36(9) Trustee Act 1925 states "where a trustee lacks capacity to exercise his functions as trustee and is also entitled in possession to some beneficial interest in the trust property, no appointment of a new trustee in his place shall be made by virtue of paragraph (b) of subsection (1) of this section unless leave to make the appointment has been given by the Court of Protection".

In these circumstances, an application will need to be made to the Court of Protection to obtain authority for the remaining trustee(s) to appoint a new trustee(s). The process is set out below.

Where P is a trustee without a beneficial interest and there is a remaining competent trustee(s) – section 36(1) Trustee Act 1925

Section 36(1) Trustee Act 1925 sets out the circumstances in which a trustee "either original or substituted, and whether appointed by a court or otherwise, is dead, or remains out of the United Kingdom for more than twelve months, or desires to be discharged from all or any of the trusts or powers reposed in or conferred on him, or refuses or is unfit to act therein, or is incapable of acting therein, or is an infant, then, subject to the restrictions imposed by this Act on the number of trustees,—

(a) the person or persons nominated for the purpose of appointing new trustees by the instrument, if any, creating the trust; or

(b) if there is no such person, or no such person able and willing to act, then the surviving or continuing trustees or trustee for the time being, or the personal representatives of the last surviving or continuing trustee;

may, by writing, appoint one or more other persons (whether or not being the persons exercising the power) to be a trustee or trustees in the place of the trustee so deceased remaining out of the United Kingdom, desiring to be discharged, refusing, or being unfit or being incapable, or being an infant, as aforesaid".

As such, where P is a trustee but without a beneficial interest in the trust, it may be possible for the remaining trustees to appoint a new trustee or trustees pursuant to section 36(1) Trustee Act 1925 in place of the incapacitated trustee. This would usually be exercised by way of deed.

Where P is a trustee without a beneficial interest and no remaining competent trustee(s) – section 41 Trustee Act 1925

Where sections 36(1) or 36(9) Trustee Act 1925 do not apply, an application can be made to the Chancery Division of the High Court to appoint a new trustee or trustees pursuant to section 41 Trustee Act 1925.

Section 41 allows the court to appoint a new trustee or trustees when "it is found inexpedient difficult or impracticable so to do without the assistance of the court". As section 41 does not automatically vest the trust assets in the new trustee(s), an application pursuant to section 54 Trustee Act 1925 may be more appropriate (see below).

Where P is a trustee without a beneficial interest and no remaining competent trustee(s) – section 20 Trusts of Land and Appointment of Trustees Act 1986

Section 20 of the Trusts of Land and Appointment of Trustees Act 1986 enables (adult and capacitous) beneficiaries to provide a written direction to appoint a trustee in place of an incapacitated trustee. It provides as follows:

"20 Appointment of substitute for trustee who lacks capacity

(1) This section applies where—

(a) a trustee lacks capacity (within the meaning of the Mental Capacity Act 2005) to exercise] his functions as trustee,

(b) there is no person who is both entitled and willing and able to appoint a trustee in place of him under section 36(1) of the Trustee Act 1925, and

(c) the beneficiaries under the trust are of full age and capacity and (taken together) are absolutely entitled to the property subject to the trust.

(2) The beneficiaries may give to—

(a) a deputy appointed for the trustee by the Court of Protection,

(b) an attorney acting for him under the authority of an enduring power of attorney or lasting power of attorney registered under the Mental Capacity Act 2005

(c) a person authorised for the purpose by the Court of Protection, a written direction to appoint by writing the person or persons specified in the direction to be a trustee or trustees in place of the incapable trustee".

Application where no capable trustee and/or vesting required – section 54 Trustee Act 1925

Where there is no continuing trustee able to appoint or apply for appointment of a new trustee or where a vesting order is required, an application must be made to the Court of Protection for it to exercise its statutory powers pursuant to section 54 of the Trustee Act 1925. This would commonly be required where all legal owners of land lack capacity and replacement trustees are required. In this situation, an application for a deputy for each person must also be being made if a deputy has not already been appointed.

Section 54 Trustee Act 1925 states:

"(1) Subject to subsection (2), the Court of Protection may not make an order, or give a direction or authority, in relation to a person who lacks capacity to exercise his functions as trustee, if the High Court may make an order to that effect under this Act.

(2) Where a person lacks capacity to exercise his functions as a trustee and a deputy is appointed for him by the Court of Protection or an application for the appointment of a deputy has been made but not determined, then, except as respects a trust which is subject to an order for administration made by the High Court, the Court of Protection shall have concurrent jurisdiction with the High Court in relation to—

(a) mortgaged property of which has become a trustee merely by reason of the mortgage having been paid off;

(b) matters consequent on the making of provision by the Court of Protection for the exercise of a power of appointing trustees or retiring from a trust;

(c) matters consequent on the making of provision by the Court of Protection for the carrying out of any contract entered into by the person concerned;

(d) property to some interest in which the person concerned is beneficially entitled but which, or some interest in which, is held by the person concerned under an express, implied or constructive trust.

The Lord Chancellor may make rules with respect to the exercise of the jurisdiction referred to in this subsection."

Trusts of land

A trust of land exists where there are two or more legal owners of property or where the legal and beneficial owners are different. In this situation, the legal and equitable interests are separated; the legal owner(s) hold the equitable interest on trust for those beneficially entitled. It is only possible for the legal title to be held as joint tenants – no severance is possible, unlike the position with the equitable interest (section 36 Law of Property Act 1925). As such, where one legal owner dies, the legal title will pass by survivorship to the remaining legal owner(s) but their estate may still have a beneficial interest if the equitable interest was held as tenants in common.

Difficulties can arise when one or more of the legal owners lacks capacity to act as a property trustee. In this situation, the process as to how to deal with the land will depend principally on three factors:

1. whether the incapable trustee has a registered enduring power of attorney or lasting power of attorney

2. whether the incapable trustee has a beneficial interest in the land

3. whether there is another competent trustee

Where P is a trustee with a beneficial interest in land and has an attorney (section 1(1) Trustee Delegation Act 1999)

If the incapable trustee has a registered enduring power of attorney (providing 1) it was dated after 29 February 2000, 2) it was dated before 1 March 2000 but it was registered before 1 March 2001 or 3) if an application made to the court for registration of the power before 1 March 2001 has not been finally refused) or a registered lasting power of attorney, and subject to any contrary restrictions in the document itself, and has a beneficial interest in the land, it will be possible for the attorney to exercise a trustee function (section 1 Trustee Delegation Act 1999).

The Trustee Delegation Act 1999 will not assist if P has no interest in the land or where there is no land.

<u>Sole surviving trustee</u>

For dispositions dated after 29 February 2000, section 7 Trustee Delegation Act 1999 provides that a receipt for capital money will overreach beneficial interests only if an attorney acts with at least one other person. Where there is a sole or sole surviving registered proprietor with a Form A restriction in the register and a transfer is executed by their joint attorneys, although two (or more) attorneys have executed the transfer they are considered to be one entity. As such, the transfer is therefore still effectively by a sole proprietor and is caught by the Form A restriction, and the overreaching provisions of the Law of Property Act 1925 are not satisfied.

In this situation, the transfer may be executed by another attorney for the donor (if one has been appointed jointly and severally) or, where the power has been registered, by an additional trustee appointed either by the other joint proprietor or by the attorney under section 8 Trustee Delegation Act 1999.

Section 8 Trustee Delegation Act 1999 (as incorporated in section 36 Trustee Act 1925) enables an attorney to appoint another trustee (and therefore satisfy the overreaching provisions) where both of the following apply:

- A person who is either—

  (a) both a trustee and attorney for the other trustee (if one other), or for both of the other trustees (if two others), under a registered power; or

  (b) attorney under a registered power for the trustee (if one) or for both or each of the trustees (if two or three) may, if subsection (6B) of this section is satisfied in relation to him, make an appointment under subsection (6)(b) of this section on behalf of the trustee or trustees (section 36(6A) Trustee Act 1925).

- This subsection is satisfied in relation to an attorney under a registered power for one or more trustees if (as attorney under the power)—

  (e) he intends to exercise any function of the trustee or trustees by virtue of section 1(1) of the Trustee Delegation Act 1999; or

  (f) he intends to exercise any function of the trustee or trustees in relation to any land, capital proceeds of a conveyance of land or income from land by virtue of its delegation to him under section 25 of this Act or the instrument (if any) creating the trust (section 26(6B) Trustee Act 1925).

The appointment can be made in the transfer itself or by separate deed.

Confirmation of beneficial interest

Where the transfer is being signed by the attorney, it is necessary for the attorney to provide a written statement within 2 months of the date of the document confirming that the donor had a beneficial interest in the property (section 2(2) of the Trustee Delegation Act 1999).

The written statement can be made separately if it is dated within 3 months of the date of the document or alternatively, and perhaps most conveniently, the written statement can be included in the disposition itself (in the additional provisions panel of a TR1 or other prescribed form, or in the body of a lease or charge):

"(Name of attorney) confirms that (donor of the power) has a beneficial interest in the property at the date of this (transfer, charge and so on)"

Alternatively, the attorney may adapt the attestation clause as follows:

"Signed as a deed by (name of donor of the power), who has a beneficial interest in the property at the date of this (transfer, charge and so on), acting by their attorney (name of attorney) in the presence of ..."

Or the attorney may expand the words of signature as follows:

"John Smith by his attorney Jane Brown who confirms that the donor has a beneficial interest in the property at the date hereof."

If the attorney cannot produce such a statement, HM Land Registry will consider other evidence that the donor had a beneficial interest at the relevant time. A statutory declaration or statement of truth (see practice guide 73: statements of truth) to that effect by a responsible person with full knowledge of the facts may be acceptable in some cases.

Vesting – section 40 Trustee Act 1925

Trust property does not automatically vest in new trustees, even if the appointment is made by deed. Section 40(4) Trustee Act 1925 specifically states automatic vesting does not apply in the following situations:

(k) to land conveyed by way of mortgage for securing money subject to the trust, except land conveyed on trust for securing debentures or debenture stock;

(l) to land held under a lease which contains any covenant, condition or agreement against assignment or disposing of the land without licence or consent, unless, prior to the execution of the deed containing expressly or impliedly the vesting declaration, the requisite licence or consent has been obtained, or unless, by virtue of any statute or rule of law, the vesting declaration, express or implied, would not operate as a breach of covenant or give rise to a forfeiture;

(m) to any share, stock, annuity or property which is only transferable in books kept by a company or other body, or in manner directed by or under an Act of Parliament.

In these situations, a vesting order will be required to transfer the legal title to the new trustee(s) and an application pursuant to section 54 Trustee Act 1925 will need to be made. Section 36 Trustee Act 1925 will not assist.

Application to the Court of Protection for the appointment or discharge of a trustee

Court of Protection Practice Direction 9F sets out the process for the following applications:

a) for the exercise of any power (including a power to consent) vested in P whether as a trustee or otherwise (section 18(1)(j) of the Mental Capacity Act 2005 (this includes section 39 Trustee Act 1925);

b) under section 36(9) of the Trustee Act 1925 for leave to appoint a new trustee in place of P;

c) under section 54 of the Trustee Act 1925 as to the court's jurisdiction;

d) under section 20 of the Trusts of Land and Appointment of Trustees Act 1996; or

e) for the court's approval of the appointment of a trustee in accordance with the terms of a trust.

Section 50(1) and paragraph 20(2) of Schedule 3 to the Mental Capacity Act 2005 and rule 8.2 of the Court of Protection Rules 2017 set out the circumstances in which permission of the Court of Protection to make an application is or is not required.

The application must be made using COP1 (and its relevant annexes, usually COP1D and COP12) and the following information must be provided as part of a COP24 (witness statement):

a) a copy of the existing trust document;

b) where relevant, a copy of any original conveyance, transfer, lease, assignment, settlement trust or will trust;

c) the names and addresses of any present trustees and details of any beneficial interest they have in the trust property. If the present trustees are not the original trustees, an explanation should be provided as to how they became trustees and copies of any deeds of appointment and retirement should be provided;

d) the full name, address and date of birth of any person proposed to replace P as a trustee, and details of that person's relationship to P;

e) confirmation that the trust is not under an order for administration in the Chancery Division;

f) if there is only one continuing trustee the applicant must confirm that both the trustee and the proposed new trustee have not made an enduring power of attorney or a lasting power of attorney in favour of the other party;

g) if an enduring power of attorney or a lasting power of attorney has been executed by a continuing trustee, a certified copy of that document must be provided. If the power has not been registered, the applicant must confirm that the trustee is still capable of carrying out his or her duties as a trustee;

h) the full name and address of any person who has an interest in any trust property as the beneficiary of a will, and whether any of them are children or persons who lack capacity;

i) if the proposed new trustee is not a solicitor or a trust corporation (for example, a bank) and has not been appointed as a deputy for the trustee lacking capacity, the applicant must provide a witness statement from a person independent of the application, wo has no interest in the trust property, attesting to the applicant's fitness to be appointed as trustee;

j) if the application relates to a transfer of assets in a will trust or similar settlement into the names of new trustees, accurate details of the trust assets must be provided (including full details of any stocks and shares held);

k) a copy of any notice of severance and evidence of service;

l) a copy of the will and grant of probate to the deceased's estate (where relevant);

m) confirmation of all relevant consents; and

n) a copy of a signed trustee's special undertaking.

Where the application relates to real property, the following additional information must be included:

a) the address of the property concerned, and whether it is freehold or leasehold;

b) the title number of the property and a copy of its entry in the Land Registry (if registered land). If the land is unregistered, the applicant should inform the court accordingly; and

c) if the property is leasehold the applicant should advise the court as to whether the applicant has a licence or consent to the assignment, and provide a copy of the same (or advise if a licence or consent is not necessary and the reason why it is not needed).

Incapacitated trustees: summary

P has capacity to retire as a trustee (and potentially appoint a replacement)	Will they consider retiring as a trustee? Usually this would be by way of deed.
The settlement makes provision for the removal of P as a trustee	Remove in accordance with the settlement. Note, a second trustee may need to be appointed.

The power of appointment or removal is vested in P	An application to the Court of Protection will be required pursuant to section 18(1)(j) MCA 2005
P needs to be removed as a trustee but no replacement necessary	An application to the Court of Protection will be required pursuant to section 39 Trustee Act 1925
Where P is a trustee with a beneficial interest and there are remaining trustees	An application to the Court of Protection will be required pursuant to section 36(9) Trustee Act 1925
Where P is a trustee without a beneficial interest and there are remaining trustees	P can be removed by deed pursuant to section 36(1) Trustee Act 1925
Where P is a trustee without a beneficial interest and there are no remaining trustees	An application to the High Court will be required pursuant to section 41 Trustee Act 1925 (but note no automatic vesting so an application to the Court of Protection pursuant to section 54 Trustee Act 1925 may be preferred)
Where P is a trustee without a beneficial interest and there are no remaining trustees	The beneficiaries (providing they are of full age, are capacitous and are absolutely entitled to the trust between them) can direct the appointment of a replacement trustee pursuant to section 20 Trusts of Land and Appointment of Trustees Act 1986

Where P is a trustee and no capable trustee and/or vesting required	An application to the Court of Protection pursuant to section 54 Trustee Act 1925 will be required but providing a deputy is appointed or an application for a deputy has been made
Where P has an attorney and has a beneficial interest in land	The attorney can exercise trustee functions pursuant to section 1(1) Trustee Delegation Act 1999 and can appoint an additional trustee if required (section 8 Trustee Delegation Act 1999)

Purchasing property on behalf of P

The attorney or deputy must be authorised to purchase property on behalf of P. There will usually be no limitations on an attorney's authority but a deputy is likely to require specific authority from the Court of Protection as the deputyship order will usually expressly exclude the power to purchase property.

Property purchased on behalf of P solely should be done so in P's name. Where the property is to be purchased jointly with another, the legal title will need to be vested in at least two trustees and a declaration of trust and Land Registry restriction (usually Form A) should be used to protect P's beneficial interest.

As noted above, a deputy cannot exercise trustee powers and as such, if the deputy is appointed as a property trustee they will be acting in that role and not as a deputy.

An application to the court for authority to purchase a property should be made using form COP1 and COP24 (setting out the reasons for the application and why the proposed purchase is in P's best interests). Forms

COP1A (supporting information for property and affairs applications) and COP3 (assessment of capacity) are not required.

Acting as a director

The role of a director is a personal appointment. It cannot be delegated to an attorney or a deputy.

Where the director lacks capacity to act as a director, it will be necessary to consult the company's articles of association in order to ascertain whether there are any specific provisions with regard to the loss of mental capacity of a director. For companies incorporated after 28 April 2013, the model articles do not provide for automatic termination of a director's appointment upon a loss of capacity but will require a registered medical practitioner to provide a written opinion to the company stating that that person has become physically or mentally incapable of acting as a director and may remain so for more than three months (paragraph 18). For companies incorporated before this date, different provisions may apply.

Where the incapacitated director was the sole director, the articles may make provision as to how a replacement director is to be appointed. This power may ultimately lie with the shareholders.

Acting as a shareholder

An attorney or deputy will usually be authorised to exercise shareholder rights on behalf of an incapacitated shareholder, even if the appointment of director has been terminated. In this situation, the terms of the deputyship order or power of attorney should be consulted, together with the articles of association and any shareholder agreement.

Where the person who has lost capacity to act was a sole director and there are no contrary provision in the articles of association, as mentioned above the attorney or deputy may be able to exercise shareholder powers on behalf of the incapacitated person in order to appoint a new director or directors.

If an application to the court is required, this should be done using form COP1 and COP24 (setting out the reasons for the application and why the authority is required and why it is in P's best interests). Forms COP1A (supporting information for property and affairs applications) and COP3 (assessment of capacity) are not required.

Statutory will applications

If a client lacks capacity to make a will, it is necessary to consider whether an application to the Court of Protection for the execution of a statutory will on behalf of the client is needed. Examples of when a statutory will application may be appropriate include:

- Where a will has been incorrectly executed and P has lost capacity to re-execute.
- Where a legacy has adeemed, for example where a specific item has been disposed of during P's lifetime. Note, however, the saving provisions of section 18 and paragraph 8 of Schedule 2 of the MCA which states that where P's property, which is not just real property, is subject to a specific legacy in P's will and has been disposed of by a deputy, the legacy will not adeem and instead will apply to the property representing the property disposed of. If the property disposed of was real property, the property representing it is to be treated, so long as it remains part of P's estate, as if it were real property. Please note that this does not apply to disposals by attorneys or by P themselves. Furthermore, given the potential difficulties with identifying the proceeds of the disposed asset, it may be appropriate for a statutory will application to still be made.

- Other examples of when a statutory will may be appropriate, include:
    - Where there has been a major change in P's circumstances or in his relationship.
    - Where an executor or principal beneficiary has predeceased P and there are no adequate replacements.
    - Where there has been financial abuse.
    - Where P's existing will or his intestacy fails to make provision for people for whom, or purposes for which, P might be expected to provide and the result of not making a will would be unjust and contrary to P's best interests.
    - Where P has re-married since he made his last will.

This list is not exhaustive and an appropriate circumstance will be entirely case specific.

The court's principal powers in respect of P's property and affairs are contained in section 18 and Schedule 2 of the MCA. Section 18(1)(i) MCA gives the court authority specifically in relation to the execution of a will on behalf of a person who lacks capacity to make one for themselves. Authority must be granted expressly; a deputy or attorney has no automatic authority to execute a will on behalf of P.

A statutory will has the same effect for all purposes as if P had the capacity to make a valid will and the will had been executed by him in the manner required by the Wills Act 1837, except to the extent that it relates to:

- the disposal of immovable property outside England and Wales, or

- insofar as it relates to any other property or matter if, when the will is executed:
    - P is domiciled outside England and Wales; and
    - under the law of P's domicile, any questions of his testamentary capacity would fall to be determined in accordance with the law of a place outside England and Wales

in those circumstances, the practitioner should seek advice from a lawyer in that jurisdiction.

All decisions made on behalf of or in respect of a person who lacks capacity, including in relation to statutory wills, must be made pursuant to the principles of the MCA as set out in section 1. In particular, the court will only authorise a statutory will if it is in P's best interests to do so. It will try to avoid becoming involved in family disputes but in *Re D (VAC v FKD)* [2010] EWHC 2159, for example, it was considered that it would not be in P's best interests for her to be remembered for having left a contentious Probate dispute to her family.

The court has also applied the "right thing" test in a number of cases, including in *Re P* [2009] EWHC 163 (Ch) where Mr Justice Lewison stated: "For many people it is in their best interests that they be remembered with affection by their family as having done the right thing by their will" and in Re M where Mr Justice Munby noted "We have an interest in being remembered as having done the "right thing", either in life, or, post-mortem, by will."

This is likely to be of less relevance where there already exists evidence of P's past and present wishes, feelings, beliefs and values, particularly where they run counter to doing the "right thing', for example in *Re JC* [2012] COPLR 540 where Senior Judge Lush noted "JC has an appalling track record. He has spent his entire lifetime doing precisely "the wrong thing" in his relationship with others…".

The cases of *Re G (TJ)* [2010] EWHC 3005 (COP) and *Re M* [2009] EWHC 2525 both consider at length the issue of best interests. In Re G(TJ) Mr Justice Morgan determined that best interests involves a number of factors, including:

- the actual wishes of P
- the beliefs and values which would be likely to influence P's decision
- other factors which P would be likely to consider if he had capacity to do so
- balance sheet of factors which P would draw up if he had capacity to do so

Although Mr Justice Morgan accepted that there will be an element of substituted judgment, he emphasised that it is absolutely clear that the ultimate test for the court is the test of best interests and not the test of substituted judgment.

It can be particularly difficult to ascertain P's best interests where P has never been able to express any relevant testamentary wishes or form any obvious beliefs and values. In *Re D (J)* [1982] Ch 237, although a pre-MCA case, Hoffman noted: "I recognise the difficulty in forming a view of what might have been expected from a person who has never enjoyed a rational; mind. But I think that in those circumstances the court must assume that she would have been a normal decent person, acting in accordance with contemporary standards of morality. In the absence of actual evidence to the contrary, no less should be assumed of any person and in this case there is nothing to displace such an assumption".

As such, there is likely to be an element of substituted judgment and given the speculative nature of establishing what factors P would be likely to consider in these types of cases, it will often be necessary to show why the intestacy provisions would be inappropriate.

Extending the consideration of best interests, Mr Justice Munby in *Re M* stated:

- There is no hierarchy between the various factors in section 4, that is, the best interests section of the MCA, beyond the overarching principle that what is determinative is the judicial evaluation of what is in P's best interests.

- The weight to be attached to the various section 4 factors will differ depending upon the individual circumstances of the particular case. A feature or factor which in one case may carry great, possibly even preponderant, weight may in another, superficially similar, case carry much less, or even very little, weight.

- There may be one or more features or factors which are of magnetic importance in influencing or even determining the outcome.

- P's wishes and feelings will be a significant factor to which the court must pay close regard. The weight to be attached to those wishes and feelings will always be case specific and fact specific and in considering the weight and importance to be attached to P's wishes and feelings the court must have regard to all the relevant circumstances. These circumstances include:

    1. The degree of P's incapacity.

    2. The strength and consistency of the views expressed by P.

    3. The possible impact on P of knowing that his wishes and feelings have not been given effect to.

    4. The extent to which P's wishes and feelings are, or are not, rational, sensible, responsible and pragmatically capable of implementation.

5. The extent to which P's wishes and feelings, if given effect, can properly be accommodated within the court's overall assessment of what is in his best interests.

Mr Justice Munby also reiterated that best interests do not cease at the moment of death and this may extend to avoiding post-death litigation.

The procedure for making an application for a statutory will can be found in Part 9 of the Court of Protection Rules 2017 and Practice Direction 9(e). The forms to be filed are:

- COP1 (application form).
- COP1A (supporting information for property and financial affairs) although this is not always required as the information is usually covered by the COP24 (witness statement). If there is any doubt, the COP1A should be included.
- COP1C (supporting information for statutory will applications)
- COP3 assessment of capacity. This must specifically address the capacity to make a will. The form focuses on the MCA test of capacity it must specifically address the *Banks v Goodfellow* test.
- COP24 witness statement containing the supporting documentation set out in Practice Direction 9(e) which includes:
    - the draft will
    - any existing will
    - any consents to act by proposed executors
    - the family tree
    - a schedule of P's assets with up-to-date valuations

  - o an up-to-date report of P's present medical condition, life expectancy and testamentary capacity

- The court fee, currently £371

Section 50(1) and paragraph 20(2) of Schedule 3 to the MCA and Rule 8.2 of the Court of Protection Rules 2017 set out the circumstances in which permission is, or is not, required to make an application for a statutory will.

Certain categories of Applicant do not require permission to apply and this includes:

- P's deputy
- The Public Guardian
- The Official Solicitor
- A donee of a Lasting Power of Attorney

The COP24 is the key part of the application and should include the information set out in Practice Direction 9(e):

(a) copy of the draft will or codicil, plus one copy;

(b) a copy of any existing will or codicil;

(c) any consents to act by proposed executors;

(d) details of P's family, preferably in the form of a family tree, including details of the full name and date of birth of each person included in the family tree. The assistance of a genealogist may be required;

(e) a schedule showing details of P's current assets, with up-to-date valuations;

(f) a schedule showing the estimated net yearly income and spending of P;

(g) a statement showing P's needs, both current and future estimates, and P's general circumstances;

(h) if P is living in National Health Service accommodation, information on whether P may be discharged to local authority accommodation, to other fee-paying accommodation or to P's own home;

(i) if the applicant considers it relevant, full details of the resources of any proposed beneficiary, and details of any likely changes if the application is successful;

(j) details of any capital gains tax, inheritance tax or income tax which may be chargeable in respect of the subject matter of the application;

(k) an explanation of the effect, if any, that the proposed changes will have on P's circumstances, preferably in the form of a 'before and after' schedule of assets and income;

(l) if appropriate, a statement of whether any land would be affected by the proposed will or settlement and if so, details of its location and title number, if applicable;

(m) where the application is for a settlement of property or for the variation of an existing settlement or trust, a draft of the proposed deed, plus one copy;

(n) a copy of any registered enduring power of attorney or lasting power of attorney. I would add to this a copy of any deputyship order;

(o) confirmation that P is a resident of England or Wales; and

(p) an up-to-date report of P's present medical condition, life expectancy, likelihood of requiring increased expenditure in the foreseeable future, and testamentary capacity.

The practitioner must also ensure:

- the COP24 addresses why the applicant is seeking the statutory will. There needs to be a good reason to depart from the terms of the current will or intestacy provisions;
- it is explained why P's circumstances have changed; and
- it is explained why the statutory will is in P's best interests. When considering best interests, the practitioner should address each element of section 4 individually, remembering there is no hierarchy or individual element of magnetic importance. Consider P's wishes and feelings by meeting with him and if the practitioner's firm has acted for P previously, consider if there is anything in the old files which indicates his past wishes and feelings, although remembering the duty of confidentiality to the client.

If the practitioner does not feel comfortable drafting the COP24, counsel can be instructed to assist with this, or with any part of the application, and the costs of this will usually be paid from P's funds.

Practice Direction 9(e) sets out the respondents and persons who must be notified of an application. The applicant must name as a respondent:

- any beneficiary under an existing will or codicil who is likely to be materially or adversely affected by the application;
- any beneficiary under a proposed will or codicil who is likely to be materially or adversely affected by the application; and

- any respective beneficiary under P's intestacy where P has no existing, or valid, will.

When considering who may fall into the categories to be served, regard should be had as to P's life expectancy, and who might foreseeably be affected by the terms of the application if P were to not die imminently.

If any of the respondents are under the age of 18, or lack capacity to conduct the proceedings, they will require a litigation friend.

A litigation friend is a person who can fairly and competently conduct proceedings on behalf of a child or a protected party (that is, a person who by reason of mental disorder is incapable of managing and administering his own affairs).

In Court of Protection proceedings, the court will consider at the earliest opportunity whether P should be joined as a party to the proceedings, and, if P is so joined, the court will consider whether the Official Solicitor should be invited to act as litigation friend, or whether some other person should be appointed to act in that role.

Rule 17.1 of the Court of Protection Rules provides that a person may act as a litigation friend on behalf of a person who lacks capacity if that person:

- can fairly and competently conduct proceedings on behalf of that person; and

- has no interests adverse to those of that person.

Usual practice is for the Official Solicitor to act as litigation friend. In *Re D* it was stated the reasons for this are:

- he can conduct the proceedings fairly and competently;

- he has no interests adverse to P's interests;

- he has considerable experience and expertise in relation to the discharge of his role as litigation friend in cases of this kind; and

- as the Official Solicitor to the Senior Court, he has a broader remit as advocate to those courts, to provide them with advice and assistance, including guidance on the impact of any decision a Judge may make.

The role of the litigation friend is considered further below.

Once the application has been issued, the court will usually make an initial directions order:

- to join P as a party

- to invite the Official Solicitor to act as litigation friend

- to direct the respondents to be served and any other persons to be notified. Respondents need to be served a full copy of the application; persons to be notified only need to be notified using form COP15.

- to direct the respondents to respond by way of COP5 and potentially COP24

- to direct the parties to report back to the court within 12 weeks to confirm whether agreement is likely, further time is required or whether the matter needs to be listed for a hearing

The requirement to serve those affected by a statutory will has been judicially described at representing "a principle of natural justice, which deters a judge from making a decision that impacts adversely on the rights of an individual without giving him the opportunity to be heard".

Rules 6.10 and 7.11 of the Court of Protection Rules 2017 permit the court to dispense with service of others and of P.

The decision to dispense with service is not a decision made by reference to P's best interests, instead "[the] decision is one made by one judge in exercise of powers given by the Court of Protection Rules. It is not an act done or a decision made on behalf of P. The principles of the Mental Capacity Act 2005 cannot be strictly applied to such a decision".

Dispensing with service will be permitted only in exceptional circumstances where there are compelling reasons for doing so. Examples of circumstances where full service may not be required include:

1. if there is only a modest departure from the status quo being proposed

2. if the applicant has taken all reasonable steps to trace the current intestate successors without success

3. the conduct of the respondent may exceptionally justify service being dispensed with, for example if the respondent had been convicted of physical or sexual abuse of P or where P's funds derive from a CICA award where P was the assailant.

Agreement to not serve P is even less likely to be agreed. The example shown on the screen does not relate to a statutory will application and extends only as to whether full disclosure of a PI settlement should be given to P.

The practitioner should assume that permission will not be granted and an application to dispense with service should be made only in exceptional circumstances.

Rule 9.12 relates to objections made by a party or someone notified of an application. If a person who has been served as a notified person or as a Respondent to the proceedings wishes to object, they should file a COP5 within 14 days of service and a COP24 within 28 days of service.

For those who are not a party to the proceedings, they can apply pursuant to Rule 9.15 of the Court of Protection Rules to be joined and this is done by filing a form COP9 and a form COP24. The COP24 should include evidence of that person's interest in the proceedings and, if that person proposes that an order different from that set out in the application form should be made, the evidence on which that person intends to rely.

The court must consider whether to join the person applying under this rule as a party to the proceedings and, if it decides to do so, it must make an order to that effect.

The parties should seek to reach agreement as amicably as possible, at the least cost to P's estate. The court may direct mediation or a dispute resolution hearing but the parties should be proactively considering this in any case. It can be useful to narrow the issues of dispute before any mediation, so as to achieve the most from the time available at the mediation (or dispute resolution hearing).

Once the order has been made, the will needs to be signed. The execution requirements are set out in paragraph 3(2) of Schedule 2 to the MCA. Those are:

- the will must state that it is signed by P acting by the authorised person;
- the will must be signed by the authorised person with the name of P and his own name, in the presence of two or more witnesses present at the same time;
- the will must be attested and subscribed by those witnesses in the presence of the authorised person; and
- it must be sealed with the official seal of the court.

Once the will has been signed, the original and two copies must be sent to the court for sealing. The court seals the original and one copy and returns both to the applicant. The applicant's solicitor is usually required to sign an undertaking to hold the will in safe custody for P's life.

If P dies before the will has been sealed, the will is still valid. *Re Hughes* ChD 8 Jan 1999 confirms that sealing is an administrative act only.

It is likely to take several months for the application to be completed, although the court does have a procedure for dealing with urgent matters. Remember that what the practitioner considers urgent may not be shared by the court and this procedure should not be used as a matter of course.

Common reasons for delay include:

1. not including all the exhibits and information required by Practice Direction 9(E) and updating it during proceedings where appropriate;
2. COP3 not addressing testamentary capacity specifically;
3. not properly identifying respondents ;
4. where P has limited cash funds, as the Official Solicitor may be unwilling to act and it can be difficult to locate another suitable litigation friend.

Conducting litigation

If P lacks capacity to conduct litigation, there are two options:

1. for someone to be authorised by the Court of Protection to conduct litigation in the name of an on behalf of P;
2. for someone to be appointed as litigation friend

No third party has an automatic right to conduct litigation on behalf of an incapacitated person.

Litigation for and on behalf of the incapacitated client

A deputy (or attorney) does not have authority to conduct litigation. Where such authority is required, an application should be made to the Court of Protection for it to exercise its powers pursuant to section 16 MCA and more specifically, section 18(1)(k) MCA (the conduct of legal proceedings in P's name or on P's behalf).

In *ACC & Ors (property and affairs deputy; recovering assets costs for legal proceedings)* [2020] EWCOP 9 (27 February 2020), the Court of Protection determined that the line between a deputy seeking advice and conducting litigation stops short of formal issue of proceedings. A deputy must be careful not act outside the terms of their authority and may be at personal risk as to costs if they do so. This also applies to attorneys.

When the court considers the application for authority to conduct litigation on behalf of P, it will need to consider some evidence of the prospects of success of the proposed litigation. It will also consider whether there should be limits to such authority. If there are concerns as to merits or costs or otherwise, the authority may be (and often is) granted only up to a specified stage of proceedings (when another merits assessment may be required), or with a limit on the costs which may be incurred without further application. The court will sometimes also do this when it is granting authority to a deputy to carry out preliminary investigations as to whether litigation should be pursued.

Where a deputy or attorney has acted without authority and subsequently seeks retrospective authorisation from the Court of Protection, they must be aware of *Re Nottley* (1839) 3 Jur (OS) 719 where it was stated "it would be very singular, indeed, that a party could find time to get up actions, and yet could not, as he alleged, find time to apply to the court for its sanction ... the petition must be refused with costs". The Senior Judge in *ACC* did not suggest that the robust approach of *Re Nottley* will always be appropriate "but there is a force in the observation that if a deputy has been able to take the urgent action, they should also be able to make the application for a retrospective authorisation hard upon its heels". In the situation of an urgent injunction being sought on P's behalf, the deputy should clearly indicate their exposure and seek urgent consideration by the court. The deputy will also need to explain why a matter was so urgent that authority could not be sought prospectively.

The Senior Judge made it clear that the court cannot give any general or prospective assurance of the outcome of any application for retrospective approval; the court's determination of applications must be made in the best interests of P.

In summary, make the application as promptly as possible and ideally before the authority is required.

The effect of the Court of Protection authorising a deputy to conduct proceedings on behalf of P is:

(a) it gives the deputy priority over others in the hierarchy of potential litigation friends for P; and

(b) it enables the deputy to use P's funds to meet the reasonable costs of the litigation and to pay a costs order made against him in the proceedings (and as such, it is usually preferable for a deputy to be granted express authority to conduct litigation by the Court of Protection, rather than being appointed as litigation friend by the court seized of the proceedings).

Litigation friend

CPR 21 and the associated Practice Direction deal with children and protected parties. A protected party is a party, or an intended party, who "lacks capacity to conduct proceedings". Capacity is determined using the test set out in the Mental Capacity Act 2005 ("MCA 2005").

CPR 21.2(1) provides that a protected party must have a litigation friend to conduct proceedings on his behalf.

CPR 21.4 deals with who may be a litigation friend without a court order. CPR 21.4(3) provides that a person may act as a litigation friend if he:

> "(a) can fairly and competently conduct proceedings on behalf of the child or protected party;
>
> (b) has no interest adverse to that of the child or protected party; and
>
> (c) where the child or protected party is a claimant, undertakes to pay any costs which the child or protected party may be ordered to pay in relation to the proceedings, subject to any right he may have to be repaid from the assets of the child or protected party".

Where no deputy has been appointed by the Court of Protection with authority to conduct proceedings, the procedure is governed by CPR 21.5(3) which provides that (where the protected person is the claimant) the person must file a certificate of suitability at the time the claim is made.

CPR 21.6 provides that the court may make an order appointing a litigation friend. An application may be made either by the person who wishes to be the litigation friend or by a party, and must be supported by evidence. The two preconditions to the exercise of the court's power under CPR 21.6 are, first whether a party is a protected party and secondly, whether the requirements of CPR 21.4(3) (set out above) are met.

In relation to capacity, Mrs Justice Falk stated that there are two elements to section 2(1) MCA 2005, namely (a) an inability to make a decision in relation to the matter and (b) that the inability is the result of an impairment or disturbance of the kind described. Section 3 MCA 2005 provides that a person is unable to make a decision for himself if he unable to understand the information relevant to that decision, retain it, use it or weigh it as part of the process of making the decision, or communicate it. As set out in *Masterman-Lister v Brutton* [2003] 1 WLR 1511 (the leading case law on capacity to conduct litigation), "the key question is whether the party is capable of understanding, with the assistance of proper explanation from legal advisers and other experts as the case may require, the issues on which his consent or decision is likely to be necessary: does he have the "capacity to understand that which he needs to understand in order to pursue or defend a claim"?".

In an article by Alex Ruck Keene, Peter Bartlett and Neil Allen, the wider issue of the role of a litigation friend is considered, particularly whether 1) a litigation friend is under a duty to act in MCA best interests (which is Mrs Justice Falk's understanding of their role – see paragraphs 67 and 75 in particular) and 2) whether (even if they are) that requires them to act as gatekeeper to determine what arguments to advance on behalf of P are. The full note can be found at https://academic.oup.com/medlaw/article/24/3/333/2733263?keytype=ref&ijkey=gsPTUKu0OSlcdfY.

Persons seeking to be appointed as litigation friend should usually seek authorisation of the Court of Protection to conduct proceedings for P and on P's behalf. The key benefit of doing so is that that it offers protection for the litigation friend against costs orders and authorises P's funds to be used to pay the costs of litigation. It is possible for retrospective authority to be obtained, although the Court of Protection may query why there is a delay in making the application. Senior Judge Hilder's judgment in *ACC & Ors* considers litigation on behalf of P in more detail.

Acting on behalf of P in relation to divorce and associated financial proceedings

Section 27 MCA prohibits anyone (attorney, deputy, the court or otherwise) from consenting to a decree of divorce being granted on the basis of two years' separation (section 27(1)(c) MCA) or consenting to a dissolution order being made in relation to a civil partnership on the basis of two years' separation. In other situations, and attorney or deputy may have authority but it will usually be appropriate for express authority of the Court of Protection to be sought.

As mentioned above, attorneys and deputies do not have authority to conduct litigation on behalf of an incapacitated person and would either need to obtain express authority from the Court of Protection to conduct litigation (authority to consent to the divorce could also be obtained as part of the same application) or for them to be appointed as litigation friend by the court seized of the proceedings. For the reasons set out above, the preferable route would be to obtain express litigation authority from the Court of Protection.

Acting as personal representative

A person entitled to act as a personal representative under Rules 20 or 22 Non-Contentious Probate Rules 1987 cannot act in that capacity if he or she lacks capacity (pursuant to the Mental Capacity Act 2005) to do so. In that situation, Rule 35 of the NCPR 1987 sets out the order of priority as to who can act.

"Where a registrar is satisfied that a person entitled to a grant is by reason of mental incapacity incapable of managing his affairs, administration for his use and benefit, limited until further representation be granted or in such other way as the registrar may direct, may be granted in the following order of priority—

(a) to the person authorised by the Court of Protection to apply for a grant;

(b) where there is no person so authorised, to the lawful attorney of the incapable person acting under a registered enduring power of attorney;

(c) where there is no such attorney entitled to act, or if the attorney shall renounce administration for the use and benefit of the

> incapable person, to the person entitled to the residuary estate of the deceased."

Person authorised by the Court of Protection

Specific authority to apply for a grant on behalf of an incapacitated personal representative must be obtained from the Court of Protection – a standard deputyship order is insufficient – and the order will need to be produced with the application for the grant.

Notice to the Court of Protection

Where a person lacks capacity to act as a personal representative and no specific authorisation has been given to another to apply for the grant, notice must be given to the Court of Protection of the intended application for a discretionary grant.

Medical certificate

Where an application is being made pursuant to Rule 35(2)(c) NCPR, a medical certificate confirming incapacity will usually be required in the following form:

[name of practitioner and/or institution]

[name of patient]

I certify that:

The above-named patient [who is now residing in this institution] suffers from an impairment of, or a disturbance in the functioning of, the mind or brain as a result of which he is unable to make a decision for himself in relation to making an application for a grant representation and administration of the estate of [name] and in my opinion he lacks capacity to manage his property and affairs within the meaning of the Mental Capacity Act 2005.

Date:

(signed)

[name]

Alternatively, a form of medical certificate (PA14) can be used. This can be downloaded from www.gov.uk/government/publications/form-pa14-medical-certificate-probate.

Authority of attorneys and deputies

The practitioner must check the terms of the Court of Protection order or power of attorney to ensure they are receiving instructions from an authorised party and what is being proposed is within the authority of that party.

Attorneys and deputies can be appointed to act:

- solely
- jointly
- jointly and severally
- under a LPA or as a deputy, jointly for some matters and jointly and severally for others

Where the appointment is joint, the practitioner must obtain instructions from all attorneys or deputies. If one has died or lost capacity, the power of attorney or deputyship order will fail. Where the appointment is joint and several, it is best practice to take instructions from all attorneys or deputies.

CHAPTER FIVE

ACC & ORS (PROPERTY AND AFFAIRS DEPUTY; RECOVERING ASSETS COSTS FOR LEGAL PROCEEDINGS) [2020] EWCOP 9 (27 FEBRUARY 2020)

A key judgment for practitioners is that of *Re ACC*. The proceedings concerned three individuals whose property and affairs deputy was in some way part of the same firm of solicitors. The common issue in each matter was whether, and in what circumstances, 1) the deputy can recover from the protected person's assets costs which have been or are likely to be incurred in legal proceedings, and 2) when may a professional deputy instruct a legal firm with which it is associated, and recover the costs from P.

These proceedings arose because the court had concerns as to what the applicants considered a reasonable interpretation of 'general' authority. Ultimately, Senior Judge Hilder determined that 'general' authority is not susceptible to exhaustive definition.

The senior judge set out and answered nine individual questions, with the most relevant determinations being as follows:

1. HHJ Hilder determined that if the authority of a deputy is to extend to conducting litigation on behalf of P, such authority must be specifically granted. The 'general' authority granted in a standard deputyship order does not encompass authority to conduct litigation on behalf of P.

2. In HHJ Hilder's judgment, she considered that it is appropriate and practicable that the 'general' authority of a property and

affairs deputy is understood to extend as far as permitting an application to the Court of Protection to draw to the attention of the court a need for consideration for welfare issues. However, in her judgment, there is no basis for concluding that it should extend as far as permitting the conduct of welfare proceedings in the Court of Protection on behalf of P without specific authority. As such, a property and affairs deputy is required to obtain specific authority to conduct welfare proceedings in the Court of Protection.

The Senior Judge did state, however, that where the responsible body does not take action (for example a local authority or integrated care board), there is a requirement on the property and affairs deputy to bring the need for welfare proceedings to the attention of the court (extending the decision of Mr Justice Charles in Staffordshire County Council v SRK & Anor [2016] EWCOP 27).

3. 'General' authority does not encompass unexceptional non-contentious tasks; authority to do an act on behalf of P encompasses such ordinary legal tasks short of taking proceedings as are an ancillary part of giving effect to that authority.

4. Although the conduct of proceedings requires specific authorisation the Senior Judge recognised that there is scope for concluding that 'general' authority includes authority to take some advice in respect of some contentious litigation.

5. Where is the line drawn between seeking advice and conducting litigation? HHJ Hilder determined that it stops short of formal issue of proceedings.

6. With regard to urgent matters, the court cannot give any general and prospective assurance of the outcome of any application for retrospective approval; the court's determination of applications must be made in the best interests of P.

7. In her judgment, the Senior Judge stated that a proportionate and required approach to addressing conflicts of interest is required and these are set out in detail in the judgment. In summary, these are:

    a. Consider whether an internal referral may be needed and ask for authority as part of the initial deputyship application;

    b. If no authority has been granted:

        i. Obtain three quotes for the work required, one may be from your own firm;

        ii. If the best interests decision is to instruct your own firm and the anticipated costs are to exceed £2,000 (plus VAT and disbursements), you will need court approval;

        iii. If the best interests decision to instruct your own firm and the anticipated costs are under £2,000 (plus VAT and disbursements), you must ensure you fully document your decision making process and ensure the annual report contains a breakdown of the fees incurred.

    Failure to comply with the above may be considered a potential breach of fiduciary duty.

8. If a person has capacity to give instructions for a specific piece of work, they will also have capacity to agree the costs in question.

CHAPTER SIX

MAKING THE APPLICATION

Court of Protection Practice Direction 9D sets out the procedure to be followed in respect of applications being made by existing deputies and attorneys.

The application is made using forms COP1, COP1E and COP24, together with the court fee of £371. If you are making an application in relation to health and welfare, you should use forms COP1, COP1B and COP3.

Your COP24 is the basis of the application and depending on what authority you're specifically seeking, you will need to adapt it accordingly. All applications should include:

- An explanation as to why the proposed course of action is in P's best interests. When considering best interests, you should address each element of section 4 of the MCA individually, remembering there is no hierarchy or individual element of magnetic importance. Consider P's wishes and feelings by meeting with him and if your firm has acted for P previously, consider if there is anything in the old files which indicates his past wishes and feelings but remembering your duty of confidentiality.

- Attach preliminary expert advice, for example where you are seeking authority to challenge an NHS Continuing Healthcare claim.

- Indicate any urgency to the application and any costs exposure to the applicant.

CHAPTER SEVEN

COSTS AND FEES IN THE COURT OF PROTECTION

Court of Protection fees

As at 1 September 2021, the fees charged by the Court are set out in the Schedule to the Court of Protection Fees Order 2007 (SI 2007/1745) (as amended):

- Application fee – £371
- Appeal fee – £234
- Hearing fee – £494
- Copy of a document fee – £5

An application fee is payable on the making of any application under Part 9 of the Court of Protection Rules 2017. This applies to all applications, whether made by deputies, attorneys, donees or other persons. An application fee is also payable on an application for permission although, if permission is given, it is not payable again on the making of the application.

No fee is payable on the following applications:

- where an application is made within the proceedings on an application notice (Part 10 of the CoPR 2017 procedure);

- on a first application where an application for permission has been made and permission has been granted (art 4(2));
- where a person who has been served with or notified of an application and wishes to take part in proceedings (under rule 9.12 of the CoPR 2017);
- where an application is made under rule 9.7 of the CoPR 2017 by the donee or a person named in a lasting power of attorney (LPA) and the application is solely in respect of an objection to the registration of the LPA;
- where an application is made under rule 9.7 of the Court of Protection Rules 2017 by the donee or a person named in a lasting power of attorney (LPA) and the application is solely in respect of an objection to the registration of the LPA;
- where an application is made under rule 9.8 of the CoPR 2017 by a donor, attorney or notified person and the application is solely in respect of an objection to the registration of an enduring power of attorney (EPA);
- where the application is made by the Public Guardian; and
- where P dies within five days of an application being made (art 4(5)).

Furthermore, it was announced on 1 December 2020 that court fees in relation to applications made for access to Child Trust Funds may be waived in some circumstances. See https://www.gov.uk/government/news/child-trust-fund-court-fees-waived-for-parents for more information.

Exemption and remission

If P is entitled to a 'qualifying benefit' (except where P is also entitled to a personal injury award) then the fee payable is remitted in full. The Court of Protection remission policy is also extended to cases where P is not in receipt of a 'qualifying benefit' but has a gross income below £16,500. Depending on the level of P's income, fees may be remitted in whole or in part as follows:

Income	*Percentage of fee remitted*
Up to £12,000	No fee payable
£12,001 to £13,500	75% remission
£13,501 to £15,000	50% remission
£15,001 to £16,500	25% remission
Over £16,500	No remission – the full fee is payable

The Court may also exercise its discretion within the scope of article 9 to remit fees where payment may cause P undue hardship.

Further details and the remission application form (form COP44A) can be found at www.gov.uk/government/publications/apply-for-help-with-court-of-protection-fees-form-cop44a.

Solicitors' costs

Costs in proceedings – the general rule

Costs incurred in any proceedings are governed by Part 19 of the Court of Protection Rules 2017 in addition to Parts 44, 47 and 48 of the Civil Procedure Rules. Rule 19.2 sets out the following general rule in relation to property and affairs applications:

"Where the proceedings concern P's property and affairs the general rule is that the costs of the proceedings or of that part of the proceedings that concerns P's property and affairs, shall be paid by P or charged to his estate".

Rule 19.3 deals with personal welfare applications and the general rule is that there will be no order as to the costs of the proceedings or of that part of the proceedings that concerns P's personal welfare.

Rule 19.5 allows the court to depart from the general rule 'if the circumstances so justify'. The court must have regard to all the circumstances, including the conduct of the parties, whether a party has succeeded on part of his case, even if he has not been wholly successful; and the role of any public body involved in the proceedings. Rule 19.5(2) defines conduct of the parties as including:

(a) conduct before, as well as during, the proceedings;

(b) whether it was reasonable for a party to raise, pursue or contest a particular issue;

(c) the manner in which a party has made or responded to an application or a particular issue; and

(d) whether a party who has succeeded in his application or response to an application, in whole or in part, exaggerated any matter contained in his application or response.

The standard provision for costs in relation to deputyship applications and ongoing costs is as follows:

> *"The deputy is entitled to receive fixed costs in relation to this application, and to receive costs for the general management of [P]'s affairs [at the public authority/solicitors' rate]. If the deputy would prefer the costs to be assessed, this order is to be treated as authority to the Senior Court's Costs Office to carry out a detailed assessment on the standard basis".*

Professional applicants should consider asking for specific authority to raise an interim bill as part of the final deputyship (or other) order in relation to the application (as opposed to general management costs as set out above). It should not be used for straightforward applications and the applicant will need to explain why the provision is required. The court will only grant the other if it is considered in P's best interests to do so. The following wording should be used as part of the main application:

<u>Deputyship applications</u>

> *"The deputy is entitled to receive fixed costs in relation to this application, and to receive fixed costs in relation to the general management of [P's] affairs. If the deputy would prefer the costs to be assessed, the order is to be treated as authority to the Senior Court Costs Office to carry out a detailed assessment on a standard basis.*
>
> *Where the deputy elects for detailed assessment of the application costs, the deputy may take payment on account up to 75% of the estimated costs which are proportionate and reasonable taking into account the size of the estate. The deputy must include in the first account to the Public Guardian details of the payment taken on account and the final costs certificate from the Senior Court Costs Office".*

Other applications

> *"The costs of the [deputy (as applicant)] [the parties] shall be subject to detailed assessment on the standard basis and raised and paid out of the estate of [P]. Pending such assessment taking place, the deputy shall be authorised to pay up to 75% of the [deputy's] estimated costs which are proportionate and reasonable taking into account the size of the estate. The deputy must include in their account (where provided) to the Public Guardian details of the payment taken on account and the final costs certificate from the Senior Court Costs Office".*

The following undertaking should also be provided, either in form COP24 or added to Form 4 (only relevant for deputyship applications):

> *"1. I am the Applicant in these proceedings and I make this statement in anticipation of a Directions Order being made asking me to file a witness statement in the form of an undertaking.*
>
> *2. I agree and undertake to repay [NAME] any amount of the payment on account which exceeds the amount allowed by the SCCO on assessment, should this occur."*

Solicitors' fixed costs

Court of Protection Practice Direction 19B deals with costs. Fixed costs are set as follows:

- Work up to and including the date upon which the court makes an order appointing a deputy for property and affairs – an amount not exceeding £950 (plus VAT)
- Applications under sections 36 (9) or 54 of the Trustee Act 1925 or section 20 of the Trusts of Land and Appointment of Trustees Act 1996 for the appointment of a new trustee in the place of 'P' and applications under section 18(1)(j) of the Mental Capacity Act 2005 for authority to exercise any power vested in P, whether

beneficially, or as trustee, or otherwise – an amount not exceeding £500 (plus VAT).

- Annual management fee where the court appoints a professional deputy for property and affairs, payable on the anniversary of the court order:
    - For the first year – an amount not exceeding £1,670 (plus VAT)
    - For the second and subsequent years – an amount not exceeding £1,320 (plus VAT)
    - Where the net assets of P are below £16,000, the professional deputy for property and affairs may take an annual management fee not exceeding 4.5% of P's net assets on the anniversary of the court order appointing the professional as deputy.
- Where the court appoints a professional deputy for health and welfare, the deputy may take an annual management fee not exceeding 2.5% of P's net assets on the anniversary of the court order appointing the professional as deputy for health and welfare up to a maximum of £555.
- Preparation and lodgement of a report or an account to the Public Guardian – an amount not exceeding £265 (plus VAT)
- Preparation of a Basic HMRC income tax return (bank or NS&I interest and taxable benefits, discretionary trust or estate income) on behalf of P – an amount not exceeding £250 (plus VAT)
- Preparation of a Complex HMRC income tax return (bank or NS&I interest, multiple investment portfolios, taxable benefits, one or more rental properties) on behalf of P – an amount not exceeding £600 (plus VAT)

- In cases where fixed costs are not appropriate, professionals may, if preferred, apply to the SCCO for a detailed assessment of costs. However, this does not apply if P's net assets are below £16,000 where the option for detailed assessment will only arise if the court makes a specific order for detailed assessment in relation to an estate with net assets of a value of less than £16,000.

- Where the period for which an annual management fee claimed is less than one year, for example where the deputyship comes to an end before the anniversary of appointment, then the amount claimed must be the same proportion of the applicable fee as the period bears to one year.

- Where a deputy or other person authorised by the court is selling or purchasing a property on behalf of P, the following fixed rates will apply for the legal cost of conveying the property except where the sale or purchase is by trustees in which case, the costs should be agreed with the trustees – a value element of 0.15% of the consideration wit maximum sum of £1,670 plus disbursements.

Practitioners must only charge in accordance with the terms of the order as supplemented (and where applicable) by Court of Protection Practice Direction 19B. There have been a number of reported Court of Protection judgments dealing with Court of Protection costs including *London Borough of Enfield v Matrix Deputies Limited* [2018] EWCOP 22, *The Public Guardian v Andrew Riddle (Nos 1 and 2)* [2020] EWCOP 41, *Penntrust Ltd v West Berkshire District Council & Anor* [2020] EWCOP 48 and the SCCO judgment in *PLK & Ors (Court of Protection: Costs)* [2020] EWHC B28. At the time of writing (January 2023), the Court of Protection Rules committee is also considering Practice Direction 19B with a view to implementing a number of changes.

Detailed assessment

Rule 19.6 of the Court of Protection Rules 2017, Parts 43, 44, 47 and 48 of the Civil Procedure Rules govern the assessment of solicitors' costs which is the usual way of determining the proper costs payable to a solicitor in legal proceedings. If a party is permitted costs, the order determining the application or a separate order dealing with costs will provide for costs to be assessed if fixed costs or agreed costs are not applicable. Costs are usually awarded on the standard basis and are payable from P's estate.

Where costs are payable pursuant to an order of the court, then the amount that can be charged is in accordance with the court's guidelines set out in the Guide to the Summary Assessment of Costs published by the Senior Courts Costs Office and the Guideline Hourly Rates as follows:

Categories of fee earner

(A) Solicitors with over eight years' post qualification experience including at least eight years' litigation experience.

(B) Solicitors and legal executives with over four years' post qualification experience including at least four years' litigation experience.

(C) Other solicitors and legal executives and fee earners of equivalent experience.

(D) Trainee solicitors, paralegals and other fee earners.

Rates

From 1 October 2021 the rates (showing the relevant localities) have been as follows:

Guideline hourly rates

Grade Fee earner	London 1	London 2	London 3	National 1	National 2
A	£512	£373	£282	£261	£255
B	£348	£289	£232	£218	£218
C	£270	£244	£185	£178	£177
D	£186	£139	£129	£126	£126

London 1 — Very heavy commercial and corporate work by centrally based London firms. Not restricted to any particular London postcode

London 2 — City and Central London EC1 to 4, W1, WC1, WC2 and SW1

London 3 — Outer London – All other London boroughs, plus Dartford and Gravesend

National band 1 covers:

Berkshire
Buckinghamshire
Dorset
Essex
Hampshire (and Isle of Wight)
Kent
Middlesex
Oxfordshire
Suffolk
Surrey

Sussex
Wiltshire
Birkenhead
Birmingham (Inner)
Bristol
Cambridge City
Cardiff (Inner)
Leeds (Inner) (within 2km of City Art Gallery)
Liverpool
Manchester (Central)
Newcastle City (within 2m of St Nicholas Cathedral)
Norwich City
Nottingham City
Watford
National band 2

All places not included in London 1 to 3 and National 1

At the writing of this book, a pilot scheme permitting the electronic filing of Court of Protection bill is being trialled. It is hoped that the scheme will become standard practice. Details as to how to assess Court of Protection bills https://www.judiciary.uk/guidance-and-resources/electronic-bills-in-court-of-protection-cases-pilot-in-the-senior-courts-costs-office/. For practitioners who are not experienced in dealing with assessed costs, it is recommended that a costs draftsman assists with the preparation of the bill and will be able to support you with filing it (and any appeals). There is an assessment fee of £87 payable to HMCTS. The fees of the costs lawyer would usually be recoverable as a disbursement (and paid by P).

CHAPTER EIGHT

WHO IS THE CLIENT?

Where the client lacks capacity, the client is still the client. The letter of engagement should be addressed to and signed by the attorney(s) or deputy but the letter of engagement must be clear that the client is the donor (where there is a power of attorney) or P (where there is a deputyship order).

The duty of care of a legal practitioner is to the client. Attorneys and deputies act as agents only. The relationship between agent and principal (and therefore between deputy/attorney and P/donor) carries with it fiduciary duties. If a deputy or attorney acts outside the authorisations of the deputyship order or power of attorney, he is in breach of his duties and acts at personal risk as to costs.

APPENDIX 1

RESOURCES

- Mental Capacity Act 2005
    - https://www.legislation.gov.uk/ukpga/2005/9/contents
- Mental Capacity Act 2005 Code of Practice
    - https://www.gov.uk/government/publications/mental-capacity-act-code-of-practice
- Court of Protection Rules 2017
    - https://www.legislation.gov.uk/uksi/2017/1035/contents/made
- Court of Protection Practice Directions
    - https://www.judiciary.uk/publications/court-of-protection-practice-directions/
- Office of the Public Guardian Guidance Notes
    - https://www.gov.uk/government/organisations/office-of-the-public-guardian
- Law Society Practice Note: Meeting the needs of vulnerable clients
    - https://www.lawsociety.org.uk/support-services/advice/practice-notes/meeting-the-needs-of-vulnerable-clients-july-2015/

- Everyday Decision Research Project
    - www.legalcapacity.org.uk/everyday-decisions/supported-will-making-report
- HM Land Registry Practice Guide 9: powers of attorney and registered land
    - https://www.gov.uk/government/publications/powers-of-attorney-and-registered-land/practice-guide-9-powers-of-attorney-and-registered-land

APPENDIX 2

EMAIL ADDRESSES FOR THE COURT OF PROTECTION

For all queries related to hearings:
courtofprotectionhearings@justice.gov.uk

All COP20A and COP20B forms:
cop_service@justice.gov.uk

All other emails and enquiries:
courtofprotectionenquiries@justice.gov.uk

APPENDIX 3

LETTER OF INSTRUCTION TO AN INDEPENDENT ASSESSOR

Dear Dr X

NAME OF CLIENT

DATE OF BIRTH

ADDRESS

I have been instructed by [client] to [prepare a [will] [lasting power of attorney in respect of [property and financial affairs] [and] [or] [health and welfare]]] [advise in relation to a gift].

[I am aware that [client] has been diagnosed with [dementia of mixed Alzheimer's/Vascular type]. Given this diagnosis and the nature of the instructions I have received, I should be grateful if you would carry out an assessment into [client]'s capacity to make the [will] [lasting power[s] of attorney] [gift].

The general test of capacity for our purposes is set out in the Mental Capacity Act 2005. This states that a person lacks capacity in relation to a matter if, on the balance of probabilities, the individual has an impairment of or a disturbance in the functioning of the mind or brain and the effect of this is that the individual is unable to make the specific decision at the time the decision needs to be made. A person is unable to make the decision for herself in relation to a given matter if, with appropriate assistance if necessary, the person is unable to understand the information relevant to the decision, to retain that information, to use or weigh that information as part of the process of making the decision or to communicate their decision by whatever means. A person should not be treated as unable to make a decision even if the relevant information can only be retained for a short period of time.

The Mental Capacity Act 2005 also provides that a person should not be treated as unable to make a decision unless all practicable steps to help them to do so have been taken without success, such as explaining or presenting the information in different ways, choosing a location where the person feels more at ease, choosing a time of day when the person's understanding is better, obtaining the help of a family member or postponing the decision if the disturbance or impairment is temporary. [Therefore, if you consider [client]'s capacity may fluctuate, please let me know if we should arrange our meeting for another time or date.]

I have set out the specific tests of capacity with regard to the decisions we are concerned with below.

<u>Will</u>

You need only show on the balance of probability whether [client] has or does not have a testamentary capacity, in other words, that it is more likely than not. Please would you consider the following points in particular, and indicate whether [client] understands them:

1. The nature of the act of making a will. This involves understanding that [s]he will die and that when she does the will comes into operation. Further, [s]he can change or revoke the will before [her][his] death but only for as long as [s]he has the mental capacity to do so.

2. The effect of making a will. This includes the appointment of executors, deciding who receives what, whether the gifts are outright, consequences of a depleted estate, that a beneficiary may predecease [her] [him], and the effect on any previous will.

3. The extent of the estate. This includes the amount of property or money or investments [s]he holds and the fact that some may be jointly owned, that some benefits may be payable only on [her] [his] death irrespective of [her] [his] will and that the estate may change during [her] [his] lifetime.

4. The possible claims of others. Beneficiaries may be left out because of other adequate provision, or because of personal reasons. [Client] must be aware of these reasons and the possibility that these could be challenged.

I enclose a copy of [client]'s draft will, which makes the following provisions:

1. [set out the terms of the draft will]

[client]'s present will makes the following provisions:

1. [set out the terms of the existing will]

Given the significance of the proposed changes to [client]'s will, [her] [his] medical diagnosis and the possibility of a claim being brought by [name], for example for insufficient financial provision or on the basis that [client] lacked capacity to amend [her] [his] will, the need for a detailed assessment of capacity is imperative.

<u>Lasting Power of Attorney – Property & Financial Affairs</u>

In relation to this particular decision, [client] will need to demonstrate that [s]he can answer the following questions:

1. What is a lasting power of attorney

2. Why does [s]he want to make a lasting power of attorney

3. Who is [s]he appointing as attorneys

4. Why [s]he has chosen those persons to act as [her] [his] attorneys

5. What is the nature and scope of the powers [s]he is giving to [her] [his] attorneys

Case law has also established that [client] will need to comprehend that [her] [his] attorneys will be able to assume complete authority over [her] [his] property and financial affairs and will be able to do anything with them which [s]he could have done, if [s]he is not capable of taking that particular decision [herself] [himself].

[Client] should also be able to appreciate that [her] [his] attorney's authority to make decisions will apply as soon as the lasting power of attorney is registered with the Office of the Public Guardian and will continue should [s]he lose mental capacity and that [s]he can only revoke [her] [his] lasting power of attorney while [s]he retains capacity to do so. [S]he should also understand the reasonably foreseeable consequences of making or not making the lasting power of attorney or making it on different terms or appointing different people.

Lasting Power of Attorney – Health & Welfare

The test in relation to the health and welfare lasting power of attorney is broadly as set out above, although of course it relates only to health and welfare matters. [Client] should appreciate that authority to make decisions will apply only if [s]he loses capacity to take decisions in respect of [her] [his] health and welfare and that the lasting power of attorney will enable [her] [his] attorneys to make decisions about anything that relates to [her] [his] health and welfare, for example medical matters, where [s]he should live and who [s]he should have contact with.

Gifts

The most important test on capacity to make a gift is *Re Beaney* (deceased). The judge in the case set out the following criteria for capacity to make a lifetime gift:

> "*The degree or extent of understanding required in respect of any instrument is relative to the particular transaction which it is to effect ... Thus at one extreme, if the subject-matter and value of a gift are trivial in relation to the Donor's other assets, a low degree of understanding will suffice but, at the other, if its effect is to dispose of the Donor's only asset of value and thus, for practical purposes, to pre-empt the devolution of his estate under [the Donor's] Will or ... intestacy, then the degree of understanding required is as high as that required for a Will, and the Donor must understand the claims of all potential Donees and the extent of the property to be disposed of*".

To summarise, [client] should be aware of:

1. The nature of the transaction.
2. The effect of the transaction.
3. The extent of the property.
4. The claims to which [s]he ought to give effect.

By way of background to the proposed gift, [set out background].

I should be grateful if you would consider these three separate tests when you meet with [client]. It is possible that [s]he may have sufficient capacity to enter into some but not all of the transactions and you should therefore consider each decision separately.

Please do not hesitate to contact me should you have any queries.

Yours sincerely

APPENDIX 4

DEED OF APPOINTMENT OF NEW TRUSTEE PURSUANT TO SECTION 36(1) TRUSTEE ACT 1925

THIS DEED OF APPOINTMENT AND RETIREMENT is made the day of. [year]

BETWEEN:—

(1) [NAME] of [address] ("**the Retiring Trustee**");

(2) [NAME] of [address] ("**the Continuing Trustee**")

(3) [NAME] of [address] ("**the New Trustee**");

WHEREAS:–

(1) This Deed is supplemental to a settlement dated [date] and made between [name] and [name] ("**the Settlement**").

(2) The Retiring Trustee is no longer capable of acting as trustee of the Settlement and the Continuing Trustee wishes to appoint the New Trustee to act as trustee of the Settlement jointly with the Continuing Trustee in place of the Retiring Trustee and the New Trustee has consented to act as trustee of the Settlement.

NOW THIS DEED WITNESSES as follows:—

1. In exercise of the power of appointment conferred upon him by section 36(1) Trustee Act 1925 and of every other power enabling him the Continuing Trustee hereby appoints the New Trustee to be trustee of the Settlement in place of the Retiring Trustee to act jointly with the Continuing Trustee.

2. The Retiring Trustee is hereby retired and is discharged from the trusts of the Settlement.

3. The Continuing Trustee and the New Trustee jointly and severally covenant to indemnify and keep indemnified the Retiring Trustee and [his][her] estate from and against all liability arising in respect of the Settlement or arising out of the execution of this Deed, and all costs and expenses in connection with it.]

IN WITNESS the parties hereto have executed this Deed the day and year first above written

SIGNED AND DELIVERED by)

[NAME])

in the presence of:–)

....

Signature of Witness ....

Name ....

Address ....

....

Occupation ....

SIGNED AND DELIVERED by)

[NAME])

in the presence of:–)

....

Signature of Witness ....

Name ....

Address ....

....

Occupation ....

APPENDIX 5

PRECEDENT SECTION 54 TRUSTEE ACT 1925 ORDER

IN THE COURT OF PROTECTION

No.

MENTAL CAPACITY ACT 2005

IN THE MATTER OF

[NAME]

AND

[NAME]

ORDER UNDER SECTION 54 OF

THE TRUSTEE ACT 1925

Made by

At

On

WHEREAS

(1) An application has been made by [name] of [address] and [name] of [address] for new trustees to be appointed in relation to the trusts affecting [property address] registered under Title No [number] at HM Land Registry ("the trust property").

(2) The court is satisfied that there is reason to believe that [name] and [name] lack capacity in relation to the matter and considers it in their best interests to make this order without delay.

IT IS ORDERED THAT

1. **Appointment of new trustees**

(a) [name and address] [names and address] are appointed to be the new trustees in place of [name] and [name] in relation to the trusts affecting the trust property.

(b) The property subject to the trusts does now vest in the new trustees upon the subsisting trusts.

2. **Costs and expenses**

The costs of this application are fixed and to be paid equally from the assets of [name] and [name] but if the costs exceed the fixed amount they be agreed by the trustees and in default of agreement are to be subject to a detailed assessment on the standard basis. This order is to be treated as an authority to the Senior Court Costs Office to assess these costs.

3. Right to apply for reconsideration of order

This order was made without a hearing and without notice. Any person affected by this order may apply within 21 days of the date on which the order was served to have the order set aside or varied pursuant to Rule 14.3 of the Court of Protection Rules 2017 ("the Rules"). Such application must be made on Form COP9 and in accordance with Part 10 of the Rules.

APPENDIX 6

PRECEDENT SECTION 36(9) TRUSTEE ACT 1925 ORDER

IN THE COURT OF PROTECTION

No.

MENTAL CAPACITY ACT 2005

IN THE MATTER OF

[NAME]

ORDER UNDER SECTION 36(9) OF

THE TRUSTEE ACT 1925

Made by

At

On

WHEREAS

(1) An application has been made by [name] of [address] ("the Applicant") for a new trustee to be appointed in relation to the trusts affecting [property address] registered under Title No [number] at HM Land Registry ("the trust property").

(2) The court is satisfied that [name] is unable to make various decisions in relation to a matter or matters concerning property and affairs because of an impairment of, or a disturbance in the function of, the mind or brain and that the purpose for which the order is needed cannot be as effectively achieved in a way which is less restrictive of her rights and freedom of action.

IT IS ORDERED THAT

1. **Appointment of new trustees**

Permission is granted to [name of continuing trustee] of [address] in his capacity as continuing trustee to appoint [name] of [address] [and [name] of [address] as a new trustee in place of [name] in relation to the trusts affecting the trust property.

2. **Costs and expenses**

The costs of this application are fixed and to be paid from the assets of [name] but if the costs exceed the fixed amount they be agreed by the trustees and in default of agreement are to be subject to a detailed assessment on the standard basis. This order is to be treated as an authority to the Senior Court Costs Office to assess these costs.

3. **Right to apply for reconsideration of order**

This order was made without a hearing and without notice. Any person affected by this order may apply within 21 days of the date on which the order was served to have the order set aside or varied pursuant to Rule 14.3 of the Court of Protection Rules 2017 ("the Rules"). Such application must be made on Form COP9 and in accordance with Part 10 of the Rules.

APPENDIX 7

PRECEDENT DEPUTYSHIP ORDER

IN THE COURT OF PROTECTION

No.

MENTAL CAPACITY ACT 2005

IN THE MATTER OF

[NAME]

ORDER APPOINTING A DEPUTY FOR

PROPERTY AND AFFAIRS

Made by

At

On

UPON the Court being satisfied that [name] lacks capacity to make various decisions for [himself] [herself] in relation to a matter or matters concerning [his] [her] property and affairs, and that the purpose for which this order is needed cannot be effectively achieved in a way that is less restrictive of [his] [her] rights and freedom of action.

AND UPON the Court being satisfied that [name]'s interests and position can be properly secured without being joined to these proceedings and without making any further direction concerning [name]'s participation in these proceedings.

IT IS ORDERED THAT

1. **Appointment of [deputy] [joint deputies]**

(a) [N [s] and address[es] [is] [are] appointed [jointly] [jointly and severally] as [deputy] [deputies] [("the deputy")] [("the deputies")] to make decisions on behalf of [name] that [he] [she] is unable to make for [himself] [herself] in relation to [his] [her] property and affairs, subject to any conditions or restrictions set out in this order.

(b) The appointment will last until further Order.

(c) The [deputy] [deputies] must [jointly and severally] apply the principles set out in section 1 of the Mental Capacity Act 2005 ("the Act") and have regard to the guidance in the Code of Practice to the Act.

2. **Authority of [deputy] [deputies]**

(a) The court confers general authority on the [deputy] [deputies] to take possession or control of the property and affairs of [name] and to exercise the same powers of management and investment as [he] [she] has as beneficial owner, subject to the terms and conditions set out in this order.

(b) The [deputy] [deputies] cannot purchase any freehold or leasehold property on [name]'s behalf without obtaining further authority from the court.

(c) The [deputy] [deputies] must not sell, charge or otherwise dispose of any freehold or leasehold property in which [name[has a joint beneficial interest. An order authorising the appointment of a new trustee (or trustees) in place of [name] must be obtained before any sale or disposition of the property.

(d) If the [deputy] [deputies] consider it in [name]'s best interests to do so the deputy may appoint an investment manager, who is regulated and authorised to undertake investment business, to manage [his] [her] assets on a discretionary basis under the standard terms and conditions applicable to such service from to-to-time, and to permit the investments to be held in the name of the investment manager nominee company.

(e) The [deputy] [deputies] may make provision for the needs of anyone who is related to or connected with [name] if [he] [she] provided for, or might be expected to provide for, that person's needs by doing whatever [he] [she] did, or might reasonably be expected to do, to meet those needs.

(f) The [deputy] [deputies] may (without obtaining any further authority from the court) dispose of [name]'s money and property by way of gift to any charity to which [he] [she] made, or might have been expected to make, such gifts, and, on customary occasions, to persons who are related to or connected with [him] [her], provided that the value of each such gift is not unreasonable having regard to all the circumstances and, in particular, the size of [his] [her] estate.

(g) For the purpose of giving effect to any decision the [deputy] [deputies] may execute or sign any necessary deeds or documents.

3. Reports

(a) The [deputy is] [deputies are jointly] required to keep statements, vouchers, receipts and other financial records.

(b) The [deputy must] [deputies must jointly] submit an annual report to the Public Guardian as and when required to do so.

4. Costs and expenses

The [deputy is] [deputies are] authorised to pay [law firm] fixed costs for this application, or, where the amount exceeds the fixed costs allowed, the [deputy is] [deputies are] authorised to agree the costs for making this application and to pay them from funds belonging to [name]. In default of agreement, or if the deputy or the solicitors would prefer the costs to be assessed, this order is to be treated as authority to the Senior Court Costs Office to carry out a detailed assessment on the standard basis.

6. Security

(a) The [deputy is] [deputies are jointly] required forthwith to obtain and maintain security in the sum of £[sum] in accordance with the standard requirements as to the giving of security.

(b) The [deputy] [deputies] must ensure that the level of security ordered by the court is in place before discharging any of the functions conferred by this order.

7. Notification

The [deputy] [deputies] must, within 14 days of service of this order by the court, notify [name] personally that the court has made a decision by providing [him] [her] with a notice of proceedings about you in the

Court of Protection (form COP14) and a copy of this Order. The requirement for the person effecting notification of the issue of this order to provide the court with a certificate of notification is dispensed with.

8. Right to apply for reconsideration of order

This order was made without a hearing and without notice. Any person affected by this order may apply within 21 days of the date on which this order was served to have the order set aside or varied pursuant to Rule 13.4 of the Court of Protection Rules 2017 ("the Rules"). Such application must be made on Form COP9 and in accordance with Part 10 of the Rules.

APPENDIX 8

ORDERS YOU ARE SEEKING (BOX 4.1 COP1)

Authority of deputy/ies

- A declaration that P lacks mental capacity to manage his or her affairs

- To confer general authority on the [deputy] [deputies] to take possession or control of the property and affairs of [name] and to exercise the same powers of management and investment, as [he] [she] has as beneficial owner

- The [deputy] [deputies] may make provision for the needs of anyone who is related to or connected with [name] if [he] [she] provided for, or might be expected to provide for, that person's needs by doing whatever [he] [she] did, or might reasonably be expected to do, to meet those needs

- The [deputy] [deputies] may (without obtaining any further authority from the court) dispose of [name]'s money and property by way of gift to any charity to which [he] [she] made, or might have been expected to make, such gifts, and, on customary occasions, to persons who are related to or connected with [him] [her], provided that the value of each such gift is not unreasonable having regard to all the circumstances and, in particular, the size of [his] [her] estate

- For the purpose of giving effect to any decision the [deputy] [deputies] may execute or sign any necessary deeds or documents

- To authorise the [deputy] [deputies] to sell the property of [name] known as [address of property] on the best possible terms and after payment of legal fees and other professional charges to invest the net proceeds for [name]'s benefit

- To authorise the [deputy] [deputies] to purchase and freehold or leasehold property on [name]'s behalf without obtaining further authority of the court

- Authority for the [deputy] [deputies] to take such steps as may be necessary to obtain (either alone or with a co-administrator) a grant of representation to the estate of [name] and to use the share to which [name] is entitled for [his] [her] benefit

- The [deputy is] [deputies are] authorised to pay [law firm] fixed costs for this application, or, where the amount exceeds the fixed costs allowed, the [deputy is] [deputies are] authorised to agree the costs for making this application and to pay them from funds belonging to [name]. In default of agreement, or if the deputy or the solicitors would prefer the costs to be assessed, this order is to be treated as authority to the Senior Court Costs Office to carry out a detailed assessment on the standard basis.

- The [deputy is] [deputies are] authorised, with retrospective effect as necessary, to instruct [name] to advise and assist in respect of issuing arising in connection with [detail]. In order to give effect to this authority, the [deputy is] [deputies are] authorised to use funds of [name] up to a limit of £[amount]. (For the avoidance of doubt, this authority does not extend to the issue or conduct of proceedings in respect of [name].)

- In so far as the authority granted by paragraph [number] above is retrospective, the costs already incurred by the [deputy] [deputies] shall be subject to detailed assessment by the Senior Courts Costs Office on the standard basis. The [deputy is] [deputies are] authorised to make from the funds of [name] a payment on account not exceeding 75% + VAT of the total sum authorised in paragraph [number] above, pending assessment.

- The [deputy is] [deputies are] authorised to obtain Counsel's opinion (including by conference, and including paying the costs of attendance at such conference by [name]) on matters relating to [name]. In order to give effect to this authority the [deputy is] [deputies are] authorised to use funds of [name] up to a total limit of £[amount].

- To authorise the [deputy] [deputies] to conduct proceedings in the name of and on behalf of [name] and to act therein in litigation friend in relation to [detail]

- To authorise the [deputy] [deputies] to act as litigation friend for [name] in the divorce and financial remedies proceedings and to approval any financial settlement

- To authorise the [deputy] [deputies] to conduct proceeds as litigation friend in the name of and on behalf of [name] under the Inheritance {Provision for Family and Dependents) Act 1975

- The [deputy] [deputies] be authorised to realise £[amount] by entering into an equity release scheme over the property known as [address] and prepare a trust deed to protect [name]'s beneficial interest in the property

- The [deputy] [deputies] be authorised in the name of and on behalf of [name] [jointly with] to enter into a mortgage of the [jointly owned] property with [lender] and to execute any necessary documents

APPENDIX 9

RE ACC PRECEDENT CLAUSES

- The deputy may instruct their own firm where the deputy considers this to be in the best interests of P for the following work which is related to the property and financial affairs of P and includes (say) the sale or purchase of any property, property related issues, employment issues etc etc where the value of the work on that matter [within any 12 month period] does not exceed £x and which will be subject to detailed assessment in accordance with para [ ] of this order; in the event that the likely work may exceed this sum or if further authority is required then the deputy may [within x months of this order being made] apply for such further authority as may be necessary, using COP9

- The deputy is authorised, with retrospective effect as necessary, to instruct [ ] to advise and assist in respect of issuing arising in connection with [ ]

- In order to give effect to this authority, the deputy is authorised to use funds of [ ] up to a limit of £[ ]. (For the avoidance of doubt, this authority does not extend to the issue or conduct of proceedings in respect of [ ])

- In so far as the authority granted by paragraph [ ] above is retrospective, the costs already incurred by the deputy shall be subject to detailed assessment by the Senior Courts Costs Office on the standard basis

- The costs of the [deputy (as applicant)] [the parties] shall be subject to detailed assessment on the standard basis and raised and paid out of the estate of [P]

- Pending such assessment taking place, the deputy shall be authorised to pay up to 75% of the [deputy's] estimated costs which are proportionate and reasonable taking into account the size of the estate. The deputy must include in their account (where provided) to the Public Guardian details of the payment taken on account and the final costs certificate from the Senior Court Costs Office

- The deputy is authorised to obtain counsel's opinion (including by conference, and including paying the costs of attendance at such conference by [ ]) on matters relating to [ ]

- In order to give effect to this authority the deputy is authorised to use funds of [ ] up to a total limit of £[ ]

APPENDIX 10

PRECEDENT STATUTORY WILL PROVISIONS

This is the last Will of me [NAME OF P] of [ADDRESS] acting by [NAME OF PERSON AUTHORISED] the person authorised in that behalf by an order dated the made under the Mental Capacity Act 2005.

1. [OPERATIVE PROVISIONS]

In witness of which this will is signed by me [NAME OF P] acting by [AUTHORISED PERSON] under the order mentioned above on [DATE].

SIGNED by the said

[NAME OF P]

by the said [AUTHORISED PERSON] ------------------------------

and by the said [AUTHORISED PERSON] [NAME OF P]

with her own name

pursuant to the said order in our presence and

attested by us in the presence of the said

[NAME OF AUTHORISED PERSON] ------------------------------

[NAME OF AUTHORISED PERSON]

……………………………………..

Witness Signature

……………………………………..

Witness Name

Address:

……………………………………..

……………………………………..

……………………………………..

……………………………………..

……………………………………..

Witness Signature

……………………………………..

Witness Name

Address:

……………………………………..

……………………………………..

……………………………………..

……………………………………..

Sealed with the official seal of the Court of Protection the ________ day of __________ 20____

I hereby certify that this will is an exact copy of the draft thereof as approved by the Court.

Signed..............................

Dated...............................

MORE BOOKS BY LAW BRIEF PUBLISHING

A selection of our other titles available now:-

'A Practical Guide to Parental Alienation in Private and Public Law Children Cases' by Sam King QC & Frankie Shama
'Contested Heritage – Removing Art from Land and Historic Buildings' by Richard Harwood QC, Catherine Dobson, David Sawtell
'The Limits of Separate Legal Personality: When Those Running a Company Can Be Held Personally Liable for Losses Caused to Third Parties Outside of the Company' by Dr Mike Wilkinson
'A Practical Guide to Transgender Law' by Robin Moira White & Nicola Newbegin
'Artificial Intelligence – The Practical Legal Issues (2nd Edition)' by John Buyers
'A Practical Guide to Residential Freehold Conveyancing' by Lorraine Richardson
'A Practical Guide to Pensions on Divorce for Lawyers' by Bryan Scant
'A Practical Guide to Challenging Sham Marriage Allegations in Immigration Law' by Priya Solanki
'A Practical Guide to Legal Rights in Scotland' by Sarah-Jane Macdonald
'A Practical Guide to New Build Conveyancing' by Paul Sams & Rebecca East
'A Practical Guide to Defending Barristers in Disciplinary Cases' by Marc Beaumont
'A Practical Guide to Inherited Wealth on Divorce' by Hayley Trim
'A Practical Guide to Practice Direction 12J and Domestic Abuse in Private Law Children Proceedings' by Rebecca Cross & Malvika Jaganmohan
'A Practical Guide to Confiscation and Restraint' by Narita Bahra QC, John Carl Townsend, David Winch
'A Practical Guide to the Law of Forests in Scotland' by Philip Buchan
'A Practical Guide to Health and Medical Cases in Immigration Law' by Rebecca Chapman & Miranda Butler
'A Practical Guide to Bad Character Evidence for Criminal Practitioners by Aparna Rao
'A Practical Guide to Extradition Law post-Brexit' by Myles Grandison et al

'A Practical Guide to Hoarding and Mental Health for Housing Lawyers' by Rachel Coyle
'A Practical Guide to Psychiatric Claims in Personal Injury – 2nd Edition' by Liam Ryan
'Stephens on Contractual Indemnities' by Richard Stephens
'A Practical Guide to the EU Succession Regulation' by Richard Frimston
'A Practical Guide to Solicitor and Client Costs – 2nd Edition' by Robin Dunne
'Constructive Dismissal – Practice Pointers and Principles' by Benjimin Burgher
'A Practical Guide to Religion and Belief Discrimination Claims in the Workplace' by Kashif Ali
'A Practical Guide to the Law of Medical Treatment Decisions' by Ben Troke
'Fundamental Dishonesty and QOCS in Personal Injury Proceedings: Law and Practice' by Jake Rowley
'A Practical Guide to the Law in Relation to School Exclusions' by Charlotte Hadfield & Alice de Coverley
'A Practical Guide to Divorce for the Silver Separators' by Karin Walker
'The Right to be Forgotten – The Law and Practical Issues' by Melissa Stock
'A Practical Guide to Planning Law and Rights of Way in National Parks, the Broads and AONBs' by James Maurici QC, James Neill et al
'A Practical Guide to Election Law' by Tom Tabori
'A Practical Guide to the Law in Relation to Surrogacy' by Andrew Powell
'A Practical Guide to Claims Arising from Fatal Accidents – 2nd Edition' by James Patience
'A Practical Guide to the Ownership of Employee Inventions – From Entitlement to Compensation' by James Tumbridge & Ashley Roughton
'A Practical Guide to Asbestos Claims' by Jonathan Owen & Gareth McAloon
'A Practical Guide to Stamp Duty Land Tax in England and Northern Ireland' by Suzanne O'Hara
'A Practical Guide to the Law of Farming Partnerships' by Philip Whitcomb
'Covid-19, Homeworking and the Law – The Essential Guide to Employment and GDPR Issues' by Forbes Solicitors
'Covid-19 and Criminal Law – The Essential Guide' by Ramya Nagesh
'Covid-19 and Family Law in England and Wales – The Essential Guide' by Safda Mahmood

‘A Practical Guide to the Law of Unlawful Eviction and Harassment – 2nd Edition’ by Stephanie Lovegrove
‘Covid-19, Brexit and the Law of Commercial Leases – The Essential Guide’ by Mark Shelton
‘A Practical Guide to Costs in Personal Injury Claims – 2nd Edition’ by Matthew Hoe
‘A Practical Guide to the General Data Protection Regulation (GDPR) – 2nd Edition’ by Keith Markham
‘Ellis on Credit Hire – Sixth Edition’ by Aidan Ellis & Tim Kevan
‘A Practical Guide to Working with Litigants in Person and McKenzie Friends in Family Cases’ by Stuart Barlow
‘Protecting Unregistered Brands: A Practical Guide to the Law of Passing Off’ by Lorna Brazell
‘A Practical Guide to Secondary Liability and Joint Enterprise Post-Jogee’ by Joanne Cecil & James Mehigan
‘A Practical Guide to the Pre-Action RTA Claims Protocol for Personal Injury Lawyers’ by Antonia Ford
‘A Practical Guide to Neighbour Disputes and the Law’ by Alexander Walsh
‘A Practical Guide to Forfeiture of Leases’ by Mark Shelton
‘A Practical Guide to Coercive Control for Legal Practitioners and Victims’ by Rachel Horman
‘A Practical Guide to Rights Over Airspace and Subsoil’ by Daniel Gatty
‘Tackling Disclosure in the Criminal Courts – A Practitioner’s Guide’ by Narita Bahra QC & Don Ramble
‘A Practical Guide to the Law of Driverless Cars – Second Edition’ by Alex Glassbrook, Emma Northey & Scarlett Milligan
‘A Practical Guide to TOLATA Claims’ by Greg Williams
‘A Practical Guide to Elderly Law – 2nd Edition’ by Justin Patten
‘A Practical Guide to Responding to Housing Disrepair and Unfitness Claims’ by Iain Wightwick
‘A Practical Guide to the Construction and Rectification of Wills and Trust Instruments’ by Edward Hewitt
‘A Practical Guide to the Law of Bullying and Harassment in the Workplace’ by Philip Hyland
‘How to Be a Freelance Solicitor: A Practical Guide to the SRA-Regulated Freelance Solicitor Model’ by Paul Bennett

'A Practical Guide to Prison Injury Claims' by Malcolm Johnson
'A Practical Guide to the Small Claims Track - 2nd Edition' by Dominic Bright
'A Practical Guide to Advising Clients at the Police Station' by Colin Stephen McKeown-Beaumont
'A Practical Guide to Antisocial Behaviour Injunctions' by Iain Wightwick
'Practical Mediation: A Guide for Mediators, Advocates, Advisers, Lawyers, and Students in Civil, Commercial, Business, Property, Workplace, and Employment Cases' by Jonathan Dingle with John Sephton
'The Mini-Pupillage Workbook' by David Boyle
'A Practical Guide to Crofting Law' by Brian Inkster
'A Practical Guide to Spousal Maintenance' by Liz Cowell
'A Practical Guide to the Law of Domain Names and Cybersquatting' by Andrew Clemson
'A Practical Guide to the Law of Gender Pay Gap Reporting' by Harini Iyengar
'A Practical Guide to the Rights of Grandparents in Children Proceedings' by Stuart Barlow
'NHS Whistleblowing and the Law' by Joseph England
'Employment Law and the Gig Economy' by Nigel Mackay & Annie Powell
'A Practical Guide to Noise Induced Hearing Loss (NIHL) Claims' by Andrew Mckie, Ian Skeate, Gareth McAloon
'An Introduction to Beauty Negligence Claims – A Practical Guide for the Personal Injury Practitioner' by Greg Almond
'Intercompany Agreements for Transfer Pricing Compliance' by Paul Sutton
'Zen and the Art of Mediation' by Martin Plowman
'A Practical Guide to the SRA Principles, Individual and Law Firm Codes of Conduct 2019 – What Every Law Firm Needs to Know' by Paul Bennett
'A Practical Guide to Adoption for Family Lawyers' by Graham Pegg
'A Practical Guide to Industrial Disease Claims' by Andrew Mckie & Ian Skeate
'A Practical Guide to Redundancy' by Philip Hyland
'A Practical Guide to Vicarious Liability' by Mariel Irvine
'A Practical Guide to Applications for Landlord's Consent and Variation of Leases' by Mark Shelton
'A Practical Guide to Relief from Sanctions Post-Mitchell and Denton' by Peter Causton

www.ingramcontent.com/pod product compliance
Lightning Source LLC
LaVergne TN
LVHW022055200926
848481LV00003B/921